WHY
PSYCHOTHERAPISTS
FAIL

WHY PSYCHOTHERAPISTS FAIL

Richard D. Chessick, M.D.

Science House

New York, 1971

Library of Congress Catalog Card Number: 74-133293
Standard Book Number: 87668-045-7

Manufactured in the United States of America

*You who can not wear yourselves out
By persisting to successes,
You who can only speak,
Who can not steel yourselves into reiteration;*

*You of the finer sense,
Broken against false knowledge,
You who can know at first hand,
Hated, shut in, mistrusted:*

Ezra Pound, "The Rest"

ACKNOWLEDGMENTS

I would like to thank Dr. Stanley Lesse, editor of the *American Journal of Psychotherapy,* for his continuing encouragement and support of my work over the years, and for permission to use material from various columns and papers in the *American Journal of Psychotherapy* in this book.

I wish to express special gratitude to those teachers and supervisors who have been especially instrumental in my development as a psychotherapist and teacher of psychotherapy: Eric Mist, Ph.D., Henry Sams, Ph.D., and Nathaniel Apter, M.D., from the University of Chicago; Francis Gerty, M.D., Peter Giovacchini, M.D., Kalman Gyarfas, M.D. (deceased), and Joel Handler, M.D., from the University of Illinois; and Albrecht Meyer, M.D. (deceased) from the Chicago Institute for Psychoanalysis.

I appreciate the loyal and devoted work of Catherine Chessick, who spent many long hours working on the manuscript of this book. It is impossible to acknowledge sufficiently my debt to my beloved wife, Marcia, who represents a model of patience, forbearance, and selfless devotion, and without whom my work could not have reached fruition.

CONTENTS

Adults, in their communication, have replaced the use of signals belonging to these categories by diacritically perceived semantic symbols. Adults, who have retained the capacity to make use of one or several of these usually atrophied categories of perception and communication, belong to the specially gifted. They are composers, musicians, dancers, acrobats, fliers, painters and poets, and many others, and we often think of them as "highstrung" or labile personalities. But it is true that they invariably deviate somehow from average Western man. Average Western man has elected to emphasize in his culture diacritic perception both in regard to communication with others and with himself. Introspection is discounted as unwholesome and frowned upon, so that we are hardly conscious of what goes on in us, unless we be sick. Our deeper sensations do not reach our awareness, do not become meaningful to us, we ignore and repress their messages. Indeed we are fearful of them and we betray this fear in many ways. It may be expressed directly; we find premonitions distasteful; if they happen to come true, we consider them uncanny. We try to deny them, or at least to rationalize them. . . . Therefore, far from being on the alert for autonomous changes in others, we do not even notice them and even less can we interpret them. Any animal knows as a matter of course when somebody is afraid of him, and acts without hesitation on this knowledge. Most of us are unable to duplicate this simple feat. We consider the psychiatrist a singularly gifted individual when he perceives anxiety, anger, longing, trust, in a patient unable to verbalize these affects.

René Spitz and W. Godfrey Cobliner, *The First Year of Life*

1

The Future of Psychoanalytically Oriented Psychotherapy

It has often happened in physics that an essential advance was achieved by carrying out a consistent analogy between apparently unrelated phenomena. . . .We have often seen how ideas created and developed in one branch of science were afterwards successfully applied to another. . . . The association of solved problems with those unsolved may throw new light on our difficulties by suggesting new ideas. It is easy to find a superficial analogy which really expresses nothing. But to discover some essential common features, hidden beneath a surface of external differences, to form, on this basis, a new successful theory, is important creative work.

A. Einstein and L. Infeld,
The Evolution of Physics

Common sense tells us that failure in psychotherapy is sometimes a function of the patient, sometimes a function of the psychotherapist, and sometimes both. Obviously little can be done about the initial psychodynamic structure presented by the patient at the start of treatment, although this could preclude therapeutic effort.

At present the greatest hope for improving psychotherapy is to develop optimal psychotherapists; we do have some control over this, for it is part of our responsibility as educators of new physicians.

Why do psychotherapists fail, and what is an optimal psychotherapist? Obviously, the psychotherapist should have a large measure of maturity and the potentiality for empathy and understanding other people; this can be achieved by careful selection of candidates and adequate personal psychotherapy. In his residency program, the psychotherapist must have excellent supervision and receive a thorough grounding in the biological and psychodynamic aspects of mental functioning and in the techniques of psychotherapy. Although most training programs already attempt, to a varying extent, to provide for careful selection, supervision, and education, this book will discuss what further steps can be taken.

In order to educate new psychotherapists to optimal levels, however, it is essential to know what needs to be changed and improved. I hope to demonstrate that, in order to produce optimal results in long-term intensive psychotherapy (and even in short-term treatment), an optimal psychic field must be presented by the psychotherapist to the patient. To develop this psychic field to the optimum, a *radical revision* in the education of the psychotherapist will be necessary. In addition to careful selection of candidates, good supervision, and a thorough education in the traditional fields, an *entire new area* of training should be provided. This will require approximately twice the number of hours devoted to formal training as are now given in the average program; it will be unpopular with administrators because the time for such training will probably have to come out of the routine hospital duties now required of psychiatric residents. In the interest of preparing optimal psychotherapists, traditional hospital ward work should be partly replaced with pursuits that will enable the psychotherapist to attain emotional maturity, what Jaspers calls "methodically pure procedures and formulations" (Schilpp, 1957), and a depth of perception and feeling. This can only be achieved by immersion in the arts; a knowledge of the philosophy of science and methods of research; an attitude toward people combining humanism with basic trust and optimism; and a life style that permits what Russell (1962) calls "idleness."

It is my thesis that a curious gap exists between our knowledge of what constitutes an optimal psychotherapist and the traditional methods of training, and that there must be substantial changes in psychiatric education in order to make further improvements in the practice of psychotherapy. Of the various factors that cause failure in psychotherapy, the one that can be remedied most easily is the psychic field of the psychotherapist, and this book addresses itself to such improvement.

In the early days of psychoanalysis it was thought that a "neutral," scientific approach was the optimal psychic field to present to the patient because it was like a mirror. In psychotherapy now it is generally accepted that this is an unattainable ideal; efforts to achieve an unnatural "neutrality" are experienced by the patient as cold rejection. Phrases such as "physicianly vocation" (Stone, 1961), "deep inner attitude" (Nacht, 1962), or "empathic quality between the psychiatrist and patient" (Fromm-Reichmann, 1950) imply that a vital aspect of psychotherapy is the quality of the "human encounter" (Buber, 1958) between the therapist and the patient. If the therapist could offer this human encounter, the patient would have the greatest opportunity of achieving a relationship that could motivate him toward psychic change.

There has been a tendency to ignore this problem because of the tradition that psychiatrists were medical men or scientists, and because of the pressures of hospital work and simple custodial duties. An optimal psychic field consists of a humane attitude on the part of the therapist, as well as an understanding of what he can accomplish and clarity of assumptions about his own therapeutic work (including his philosophical position on the nature of man). Jaspers (1964) has developed this concept at length, and has spoken of the necessity for the therapist to have *time* to dream:

Often I gazed out on the scenery, up at the sky, the clouds; often I would sit or recline without doing anything. Only the calmness of meditation in the unconstrained flow of the imagination allows those impulses to become effective without which all work becomes endless, non-essential, and empty. It seems to me that for the man who does not daily dream a while, his star will grow dark, that star by which all our work and everyday existence may be guided [Schilpp, 1957].

In the Middle Ages, people tried to understand the motions of heavenly bodies and projectiles, as well as other natural phenomena by comparing them with animal and human behavior. Frank (1947) calls this the "organismic conception," and it can be traced back to the teachings of Aristotle. The parallel in psychotherapy is what Zilboorg (1941) calls "The restless surrender to demonology." Emotional illness was described in terms of supernatural creatures taking possession of the body or, as in the case of hysteria, of various bodily parts or organs wandering through the body and inflicting all sorts of weird suffering on the victim. At worst, it was believed that magic spells were transmitted from witches and others to their victims, thereby inflicting their symptoms on them. As Zilboorg reports, "Epidemics of psychopathies began to appear. . . . Passions were aroused and soon instruments of torture and burning fagots became the recognized tools of psychiatry."

The renaissance in physics, embodied especially in the work of Galileo and Newton, occurred in the seventeenth century. These geniuses brought to flower what Frank calls the "mechanistic view," in which natural phenomena were explained in terms of simple machines such as levers and wheels, particles and waves. The great laws of Newton and his universal law of gravitation stand as an outstanding achievement of humanity (Manuel, 1968). It should be noted that the success of the mechanistic view was not due to any intrinsic philosophical validity, but rather to the utility of Newton's laws in understanding and predicting many hitherto confusing and seemingly unrelated phenomena.

Psychiatry made a valiant attempt to imitate the renaissance in physics and ultimately in medicine. The great systematizers and classifiers of the nineteenth century (including Kraeplin and Griesinger) built on the humane revolution of Vives, Weyer, Pinel, and

Esquirol toward the goal of recognizing emotional symptoms as an illness and with the ultimate hope of discovering pathogenic bacterial and cellular changes. In the area of neuroses, pioneer work by Charcot, Bernheim, Liebault, and Janet paved the way for Freud.

Freud was clearly attempting to provide a mechanistic model of mental phenomena, based on Newton's ideas of natural phenomena. Even a superficial study of his development from neurologist to psychoanalyst (Jones, 1953) demonstrates this, and his work stands as the monumental effort in the history of psychiatry to develop a set of general mechanical laws of mental functioning. The immediate application of his laws to hitherto poorly understood and seemingly unrelated phenomena (such as schizophrenia, Bleuler, 1950) gave Freud the status of a Newton in the field of psychiatry.

Even today, for many practical purposes, the basic Freudian theoretical constructs, including the structural theory (Arlow & Brenner, 1964) of mental functioning and the signal theory of anxiety, have been almost universally accepted by psychotherapists; his concept of the developmental stages and other cornerstones of psychotherapy such as the transference and dream interpretation remain in general use, just as for many practical purposes Newtonian physics is still quite adequate.

The status of physics at the end of the nineteenth century is comparable to the status of psychotherapy in the middle of the twentieth century. In physics at that time,

> More and more physical phenomena were discovered that could be explained only with great difficulty and in a very involved way by the principles of Newtonian mechanics. As a consequence new theories appeared in which it was not clear whether they could be derived from Newtonian mechanics, but which were accepted as temporary representations of the observed phenomena [Frank, 1947].

Thus, a new set of forerunners of a theoretical revolution began to appear. Einstein (1954) believed that the greatest of these were Hertz, Faraday, and especially Maxwell (just as Copernicus, Kepler, and Galileo were the great forerunners of Newton). Einstein said,

> Before Maxwell, people conceived of physical reality — in so far as it is supposed to represent events in nature — as material points, whose changes consist exclusively of motions, which are subject to total differential equations. After Maxwell they conceived of physical reality as represented by continuous fields, not mechanically explicable, which are subject to partial differential equations. This change in the conception of reality is the most profound and fruitful one that has come to physics since Newton; but it has at the same time to be admitted that the program has by no means been completely carried out yet.

Newton's theories were undermined by the great experimental work of Hertz, Faraday, and Maxwell (among others), and the philosophical foundations of Newtonian physics were also attacked. The noted Austrian physicist, Ernst Mach, demanded *economy of thought* in theory: the greatest possible number of observable facts should be organized under the fewest possible principles, regardless of the philosophical implications. He objected to such concepts as absolute space and absolute time which Newton had postulated in developing his laws; for these he hoped to substitute the fixed stars.

The great French mathematician, Henri Poincaré, suggested that the general propositions of science are not statements about reality but are free creations of the human mind; therefore, they cannot be judged as true or false but only as to whether they are expedient, useful, and can be experimentally verified. The extreme of this approach is known as operationalism (Bridgman, 1959) in which all scientific concepts are defined solely in terms of the operations used to measure them; no mention is made of physical reality, which is viewed as inaccessible to human knowledge.

Although Freud's theories were never so widely received as Newton's, it could easily be maintained that the high point for Freud came just after World War II. At that time, under the influence of many outstanding psychoanalysts who fled to the United States and England from continental Europe, all American and much of British psychiatry became permeated with Freudian concepts. To become a Freudian psychoanalyst in the United States in the postwar years was to attain the highest possible prestige and respect in the psychiatric profession.

This prestige ranking among psychiatrists was unfortunate because it led to excessive expectations for the therapeutic efficacy of psychoanalysis, expectations that Freud never claimed. Indeed, his final papers — for example, the magnificent *Analysis Terminable and Interminable* (1937) — were pessimistic about psychoanalysis as a treatment modality. Furthermore, the expense of psychoanalysis and the extreme difficulty in verifying the results of any prolonged psychotherapeutic procedure led to gradual disillusionment with the method; psychoanalysts tended to form societies that were isolated and beleaguered.

Again, as in the case of Newton's theories, certain illustrious forerunners of change challenged Freud's theories on the basis of their own extensive clinical or experimental material. The most incisive of these forerunners were Adler, Horney, Fromm, and Sullivan. Applying Freud's theories to various aspects of human behavior and emotional illness convinced these psychoanalysts (and many others) that Freud's theories needed to be revised. As in the case of Hertz, Faraday, and Maxwell, they made numerous controversial revisions of certain important sections of his theory. At this point it would be unreasonable to suggest an *ad hominem* argument (the kind that has become the curse of the psychoanalytic profession) since, regardless of their personal motivation, these forerunners have attracted many followers and have made an impact on the practice of psychotherapy.

There were and are major defects in Freud's theories, as in all scientific theories. The best-known defects are his anti-feminist bias (Gilman, 1971), his hopelessness about schizophrenia, and the lack of adequate provision in his original structural theory for creativity and autonomous functioning. The contributions of Adler, Horney, Fromm, and Sullivan are excellently summarized by Mullahy (1948) and Monroe (1955). Horney and Sullivan both emphasized warmth and affection in the mother-child relationship as a crucial factor in the genesis of mental illness, while Adler and Fromm stressed adaptation to or mastery of the human environment. The interactional field between the individual and his environment came to be considered important in the development of health or illness.

Adler introduced the concept of a life style and Sullivan the concept of a career line, thereby emphasizing the adaptational and interactional aspects of life as being more than just the product of "repetition compulsion." Fromm insisted that social and psychological forces interact in a circular relationship. Munroe said that Sullivan's theory was "the only 'non-libido' approach which seems to me at all comparable to Freud's approach in its theoretical potential, and I see no fundamental incompatibility between the two." At the same time, there was confusion and disagreement among the various schools of psychoanalysis, comparable to the field of physics at the end of the nineteenth century.

Just as Newton's theories were attacked from both an experimental and philosophical point of view, Freud's theories were criticized by both clinicians and philosophers. The most popular philosophical movement to challenge Freud's approach is existentialism, just as positivism was the principal philosophical movement that challenged Newton's theories. There is absolutely no similarity between existentialism and positivism; in fact, they are diametrically opposed. The basic tenets of positivism are well known, but so-called existentialism remains a confusing hodge-podge. In fact, the term "existentialism" has become meaningless although it is often used in psychiatric and philosophical literature.

When the average psychotherapist encounters the concepts of existentialism, he notes that there are a tremendous number of undefined and mysterious terms, and that it seems to be impossible for philosophers to agree on its definition.

Existentialism may be traced to three sources. The first is World War II, which represented the final blow to the idea that man is a rational animal and disillusioned many people about science as a way of solving the world's problems. The second source is the writings of certain forerunners in philosophy and literature, notably St. Augustine, Pascal, Kierkegaard, Nietzsche, and Dostoevsky, who were extremely preoccupied with their personal experiences (their feeling of existence) and tried to establish knowledge from introspection about their subjective feelings. The third source is the philosopher Edmund Husserl, who died just before World War II. In an effort to solve the Kantian dilemma between the object we know (*phenomena,* appearance) and the unknowable thing-in-itself (*noumena,* the object as it is apart from our knowing minds) and to find absolutely certain knowledge, Husserl developed what he called the "phenomenological method" (1964).

As Brennan (1967) describes this method, "We should not approach things as if they were sets of appearances with their reality lying *behind* them. Patient, careful analysis of things and events that come to us 'showing themselves' is the way of phenomenology." Jones (1969) carefully depicts the anti-scientific bias and grandiosity in Husserl's work as well as its logical and philosophical weaknesses. Husserl's "approach became entangled in his urgent personal need for absolutes, with the unfortunate result that his experientialism was converted into ontology and the data of observation were dressed up as 'objects originaliter.' " At the same time Husserl influenced the schools of sociology and psychology that followed him by insisting that psychological investigations stress the prior importance of the immediate data of our inner experiences. A thorough review of his difficult philosophy is found in Kockelmans's (1967) collection of essays. It should be noted that existentialists, beginning with Heidegger, have claimed to be influenced by or to use the phenomenological method directly. This is simply not correct and is often based on a misunderstanding of Husserl, as he himself pointed out with great disappointment.

Among the many books on the existentialist movement, I found Kaufmann (1960), Blackham (1952), and Barrett (1958) to be the most useful and clearly written. In spite of considerable chaos in the movement, the existentialist philosophers perform an important function by insisting that any study of man must consider his inner feelings, his sense of being-in-the-world, and his dread of death. Man cannot be reduced to a mechanical model; thus, by implication, the psychological illnesses of man cannot be treated mechanically according to the medical model of extirpating pathogenic agents by the doctor-authority. In spite of the poor thinking, muddled writing, and almost hysterical declarations of existentialist works, they have helped to bring about a reorientation toward human beings and human problems.

Kierkegaard, in many ways the most original and the first of the Christian existentialists, and later Martin Heidegger introduced the concept of existential anxiety. Heidegger is generally regarded as the most profound existential philosopher, although he rejected this label. His major (unfinished) work, *Being and Time* (1962), is so difficult I would recommend that the reader begin with Gelven's (1970) exposition of it. To understand Heidegger's thought, the interested reader can consult Grene (1957), Naess (1968), and Schmitt (1969). Heidegger's work has been severely criticized on many grounds and described as anti-rational, anti-scientific poetry. (In another publication [Chessick, 1971b], I have investigated the grounds of Heidegger's approach to human Being.)

Although Heidegger produced an almost untranslatable and unreadable theoretical work that was never finished, it profoundly influenced many thinkers in continental Europe. Each thinker interpreted or misinterpreted Heidegger to suit himself; however, two groups of philosophers can generally be delineated. The first group (the theistic and sometimes Christian existentialists) borrowed from Heidegger, or Kierkegaard, or both, using man's absurd plight as a springboard for theistic and sometimes traditional religious faith. These thinkers include Jaspers, Marcel, Tillich, and Unamuno (who was almost convinced). The second group (the humanistic and sometimes atheist existentialists) used man's alone-ness in the world, his despair and fear of death, and his inability to know *noumena* as the basic principles of their philosophical systems. The most famous of this group are Sartre, Ortega y Gasset, and Camus; the latter might be called the Dostoevski of this group because of his magnificent literary portrayals of the atheistic, alienated man.

Friedman (1955) points out how Martin Buber's thought from

1900 to 1923 moved from mysticism to existentialism to dialogical philosophy, culminating in the publication of *I and Thou* (1958). Buber's stress on the importance of simple immediacy and the meaningful relationship between human beings was conceived as another philosophical method to obtain knowledge, but it had obvious and immediate ramifications for the practice of psychotherapy, especially in our present alienated age, and for the treatment of borderline patients (Farber, 1957).

Borrowing from all these philosophers, psychiatrists in continental Europe formulated something called "existential psychiatry." In fact Jaspers (a professional psychiatrist) and Sartre, who were both essentially philosophers, established psychiatric systems based on their philosophy. The adoption by psychiatrists of the various notions of the existentialist philosophers is well illustrated by May (1958) in a volume that contains contributions by some of the best-known existential psychiatrists. A recent book by Weigert (1970) illustrates how the concept of "I — Thou," the language of Heidegger, and — unfortunately — the usual misinterpretation of Husserl, have been incorporated into psychoanalytic thinking.

It should be emphasized that any careful review of existentialist psychotherapy reveals not so much a change in psychotherapeutic technique as a change in the *attitude* of the psychotherapist toward the patient. This parallels the change in attitude towards the data of physical experiments signaled by Mach and Poincaré, and later elaborated by Einstein.

Returning now to physics at the end of the nineteenth century, we have seen how Newton's theories were under attack from two directions. Experimental data appeared that could only be fitted into Newton's theories by tortuous reasoning. The philosophical basis of Newton's laws, which depended upon ideas of absolute space and absolute time, was being torn away by thinkers who had no respect for immutable absolutes.

Two conflicting new orientations and new methods appeared, posing differences that have not been resolved in physics to this day; they have led to a continuing quarrel about theoretical representations of reality and a divergence in experimental interests. The first of these was the quantum theory, as described by Einstein and Infeld (1938):

> Quantum physics formulates laws governing crowds and not individuals. Not properties but probabilities are described, not laws disclosing the future of systems are formulated, but laws governing the changes in time of the probabilities and relating to great congregations of individuals.

The famous principle of Heisenberg made it clear that, according to quantum mechanics, it was impossible to separate the observer from the observed in studying a given particle. Thus, it was necessary to have statistics of groups that would, describe only probabilities, but without control or prediction for any given individual in the group.

Einstein, defending the second orientation, could never satisfy himself with this statistical kind of representation of the reality of physics:

> I am still inclined to the view that physicists will not in the long run content themselves with that sort of indirect description of the real . . . . We shall then, I feel sure, have to return to the attempt to carry out the program which may be described properly as the Maxwellian — namely the description of physical reality in terms of fields which satisfy partial differential equations without singularities [1954].

And he coined the aphorism "I cannot believe that God would play dice with the universe," in sharp disagreement with the quantum theory. This dispute is described by Heisenberg (1971).

Einstein's approach was in the tradition of Newton and Maxwell. He brought the field theory to fruition, although he did not accomplish his ultimate aim — a unified field theory, from which

all experimental phenomena in physics could be predicted —
at least not to the satisfaction of many physicists. I would like to
emphasize Einstein's approach or *attitude,* described by Einstein
and Infeld (1938):

> In nearly every detective novel since the admirable stories of
> Conan Doyle there comes a time where the investigator has
> collected all the facts he needs for at least some phase of his
> problem. These facts often seem quite strange, incoherent, and
> wholly unrelated. The great detective, however, realizes that
> no further investigation is needed at the moment, and that
> only pure thinking will lead to a correlation of the facts collect-
> ed. So he plays his violin, or lounges in his armchair enjoying
> a pipe, when suddenly, by Jove, he has it! Not only does he
> have an explanation for the clews at hand, but he knows that
> certain other events must have happened. Since he now knows
> exactly where to look for it, he may go out, if he likes, to
> collect further confirmation for his theory.
>
> The scientist reading the book of nature, if we may be
> allowed to repeat the trite phrase, must find the solution for
> himself, for he cannot, as impatient readers of other stories
> often do, turn to the end of the book. . . . To obtain even a
> partial solution the scientist must collect the unordered facts
> available and make them coherent and understandable by
> creative thought.

Einstein also demonstrated two important personality charac-
teristics that are often linked with the creative attitude: humanism,
manifested by his sympathy and tolerance for all people; and
optimism, manifested by his belief that problems could (and
eventually would) be solved and his belief in the rationality of
nature.

Incidentally, much can be learned from Einstein's way of life.
His frugality and simplicity allowed him the time and peace of mind
to pursue creative interests. His views about research have been
largely ignored; he felt that one should not be paid for doing
research, but only for teaching (a "cobbler's trade") — a concrete

contribution. He believed that research should be done in one's spare time or leisure. Leisure or idleness (Russell, 1962) gives one the time to do research in an unhurried, creative fashion without the pressure to produce. Research done under these conditions would put an end to the forced publication of much nonsense that paid researchers do in order to demonstrate to the authorities that they are producing something for the money they are receiving. If only the academic world would pay attention to Einstein!

The discipline of psychotherapy today stands where physics was at the beginning of this century. Recent developments in the psychotherapy of groups, families, and married couples parallel the development of quantum mechanics and constitute an important area of investigation. Since there are no theoretical formulations comparable to the mathematics of probability that can be applied to clinical group situations, we must admit that this aspect of psychotherapy is only in its scientific infancy. Because group psychotherapies lack both a scientific basis and a theoretical construction, they are unfortunately quite prone to charlatanism. The development of a unified field theory for psychotherapy that could encompass both the phenomena of individual and group behavior is a future goal.

The best theoretical formulation at present for individual psychotherapy — the Freudian (with or without neo-Freudian revisions) — is now being attacked clinically and philosophically. Hartmann, Kris, and Lowenstein have altered Freud's structural theory within his own framework (Hartmann, 1958).

Schafer (1970), in reviewing Hartmann's contributions, points out that "the chief questioners of the commitment to the natural-science model have been the existential analysts." If individual psychotherapy follows the route of physics, it will not go far in the direction of existentialism. Existentialist theories are muddled and confused, and the practicing psychotherapist cannot use them without sacrificing depth and winding up with mere catch phrases and slogans. It seems that at present the existentialists in psychotherapy are clinging to their version of phenomenology, refusing to separate subject and object (thereby adopting an anti-scientific bias). As May (1958) states: "Kierkegaard foretells the viewpoint of

Bohr, Heisenberg, and other contemporary physicists that the Copernican view that nature can be separated from man is no longer tenable." Similarly, Barrett (1959) points out that Heidegger's theory of man is a "field theory" in that man has no demarcated ego separated from his world, and Barrett tries to make an analogy with Einstein's theories. However, such a comparison produces a misunderstanding of both Heidegger and Einstein. Heidegger is presenting a theory of "human being" (*dasein*) as an approach to the question "What is Being?" *not* a theory of personal human existence. He sees human being as being completely immersed in the world; this is not a "theory of man" in the usual sense. (It is, as Barrett suggests in parentheses, a theory of Being.)

More important, Einstein saw mass and energy *both* as manifestations of the same fundamental entity, and he believed that both could eventually be pinned down and discussed for individual entities, not only for groups of entities as in quantum theory. Heidegger, Jaspers, and Buber have all put forth important ideas on the interaction of man with man; unfortunately, their ideas are bogged down in complex metaphysical, mystical, or poetic superstructures and these must be cleared away for the purposes of clinical psychotherapeutic work. A new general theory of therapy would have to include the basic conceptions of Freud (just as Einstein's field equations can be resolved into Newtonian physics in special situations) but focus more on the human interaction or encounter in psychotherapy.

I believe psychotherapy will go in the direction Einstein has already taken physics, although no one comparable has appeared on the horizon in psychotherapy. A beginning, however, has been made in a little-known paper by Eissler (1943) on the psychotherapy of schizophrenia. He wonders why, in the light of advancement in the understanding of the psychodynamics of schizophrenia, so little has been accomplished in the psychotherapy of schizophrenia. He writes:

The starting point of the thesis of this paper is the assumption that the majority of those patients who are classified as schizophrenics at present could be cured by means of psychotherapy without gross interference with their physical condition, if an adequate psychic field could be established. By this term is meant a configuration of stimuli to which a personality structure reacts in such a way as to satisfy a desire or to perform an integrative act or to decrease pent-up tension.

In view of the structure of schizophrenia the adequate psychic field is bound to be a specific constellation in another human being. The establishment of this specific constellation, to be sure, is not the only step necessary in the therapeutic process. But once the adequate psychic field has been established, the opportunity for reconstruction is given . . . . Hence it is permissible to assume that the difficulty in the therapy of the schizophrenic psychoses is not merely the patient's disease, but predominantly involves certain limitations in the personality of those who try to apply therapy. These limitations consist in the inability of the therapist to establish in himself that dynamic situation to which the schizophrenic would respond if it were offered to him.

The trend in psychodynamic psychotherapy since the time of Freud has been to emphasize and understand the therapeutic aspects of the relationship between psychotherapist and patient. In this relationship the psychic field and the attitude of the psychotherapist are crucial. The psychotherapist must have inborn talent, good supervision, and a thorough knowledge of psychodynamics and psychotherapeutic technique; he must also be an "idle" man in order to indulge his scientific curiosity: "Medical men will have time to learn about the progress of medicine, teachers will not be exasperatedly struggling to teach by routine methods things which they learnt in their youth . . . . Above all there will be happiness and joy of life, instead of frayed nerves, weariness and dyspepsia" (Russell, 1962). In present-day psychiatric education, "frayed nerves, weariness and dyspepsia" seems to be the rule for both residents and their teachers.

Reflection requires much knowledge. The psychotherapist, to become relatively wise and mature, must understand something about history, philosophy, ethics, philosophy of science, psychology, anthropology, and sociology. He must learn about people not only from personal experience and seminars but from art and literature, which, of course, necessitates time to read and reflect. He must become a human being in the optimal sense of the word before he can offer the best possible human encounter to his patients.

One of the most important psychiatrists of our time, Karl Jaspers (Schilpp, 1957), has emphasized the advantage of not being burdened down with routine hospital duties. Because of a physical illness, he could not assume routine duties in his psychiatric training. He writes:

> The disadvantage of my position became an advantage. I could see and investigate everything without having my time occupied by routine duties. Besides carrying on my own investigations, I did not have a single patient from whose case I did not learn and remember something. I watched what my colleagues were doing, reflected on their procedures and my own, raised them to a higher level of conscious awareness, criticised them and pushed on to methodically pure procedures and formulations.

In conclusion, the greatest hope for preventing failure in psychotherapy lies in improving psychotherapists. Toward this end, I have attempted to review past developments in psychotherapy, and to assess future possibilities. I have reviewed the history of physics, in the hope that it may offer a parallel with the development of psychotherapy. Since physics has been the most eminently successful science of our time, we hope our discipline may emulate physics. Certain parallels do exist: both began in the Middle Ages with an organic or demonological set of explanations for phenomena. This gave way to a mechanistic explanation, brought to ultimate fruition by Newton in physics and Freud in psychotherapy. Newton's theories were undermined by experimental data that could not be fitted into the theory and by a recognition of the weakness of the philosophical underpinnings of the theory. Freud's theories have come under a similar attack.

Finally, Newton's theories were replaced by the quantum mechanics of the behavior of aggregates of particles on the one hand, and by Einstein and Maxwell's field theories on the other, which led to spectacular advances in physics. No Einstein has appeared in our field, but psychotherapy is presently splitting into the group therapies on the one hand and new directions in individual therapy on the other.

In individual therapy it is becoming clear that an optimal psychic field must be presented to the patient by the therapist. This will obviously require talented individuals; good supervision and adequate training in psychodynamics and therapeutic technique; and humane, optimistic, and mature individuals with the leisure to create and to promote empathy and interest in their patients. Clearly, a much more thorough commitment of time and effort will be necessary even during psychiatric residency training.

2

Education of the Psychotherapist

> It seems to me that what is most important . . . is not so much
> what the analyst says as what he is. It is precisely what he is
> in the depths of himself — his real availability, his receptivity
> and his authentic acceptance of what the other is — which
> gives value, pungency and effectiveness to what he says . . . .
> The communication from one unconscious to another which
> becomes established in the transference relationship between
> therapist and patient permits the latter to perceive the pro-
> found benevolent attitude of the physician.
>
> S. Nacht,
> *"Reflections on the Evolution of Psychoanalytic Knowledge"*

Modern psychotherapy is based on certain premises that were
first suggested by Freud and that (with modifications) are still
pertinent. That is to say, psychotherapy must deal with the basic
pattern of attitudes and feelings derived from the mother-infant
symbiosis and later incorporated into a nuclear personality through
further childhood experiences with mother, father, siblings, and
others. According to Saul (1958): "The child we once were lives on

in each of us however much of the rest of the personality matures." Mental illness is caused by the unhealthy development of ego functions — a warp in the childhood core; everyday miseries cannot be effectively dealt with because of the perpetual interference of the childhood nucleus. The disorder among the functioning parts of the personality leads to the failure of relationships between the individual and other people.

Further experiences in later life with significant people can ameliorate or cover over those warps in the ego functions that developed early in life, but only the most unusual experiences can reach back and substantially change the childhood nucleus within the personality. The most important of these experiences is the intense interaction of long-term uncovering psychotherapy. We can say that this process has cured a patient only when there has been a fundamental change in the childhood core of the personality, which is reflected in substantial and permanent improvement in ego function. (This is discussed in detail in Chessick, 1969a).

Although a variety of group and individual psychotherapy techniques have been developed in the past decade to deal with symptoms of mental illness with varying degrees of success, this neither contradicts nor negates these basic premises. Unfortunately, three factors have obscured the situation. First, it is much easier to evaluate certain of the new techniques aimed at symptom relief statistically, leading to the erroneous implication that some of them are scientific whereas long-term uncovering psychotherapy is not. Second, some of the techniques have a certain fad-appeal, especially to practitioners who want to avoid the arduous training necessary to do long-term uncovering psychotherapy and to patients who need to maintain their defences for various reasons. Third, the sheer frustration of the long and arduous process of intensive uncovering psychotherapy, even if successful, leads us to seek shortcuts, perhaps grasping at fads and straws.

What is obsolete in psychotherapy is not the process itself, which still remains our best curative technique, but rather the spirit of "Consciousness I" (Reich, 1970) that unfortunately pervades American medical practice. In its most extreme, nineteenth-century form, this doctrine holds that it is a dog-eat-dog world, that every man must look out for himself, that "the game is winning and getting rich and powerful, and nothing else, and that no higher community exists beyond each individual's selfish appraisal of his interests" (Reich, 1970).

Numerous studies (including Hollingshead and Redlich, 1958) have shown that in American medical practice the quality of care depends upon the patient's socioeconomic status; nowhere is this more true than in psychiatry, and all private practitioners are aware of this. Except for those lucky psychiatrists with social connections who receive a steady stream of referrals from the wealthy, most of us are constantly faced with the necessity of modifying our treatment program to fit the purse of the patient. I think (if we were honest) we would have to admit that the most important determinant of whether a patient receives individual long-term uncovering psychotherapy or not is not an assessment of his ego functions or capacity to respond to treatment, but whether he has the time and money for this costly and time-consuming process. These criteria for deciding are obsolete and must be changed. It is one thing to argue that a patient must make some sacrifice of time and money for psychotherapy, but the burdens of uncovering psychotherapy are simply beyond the financial capacities of the entire lower class and most of the middle class.

We all know doctors, clergymen, lawyers, school teachers, nurses, social workers, and others in the helping professions who could become much more effective in their work if they were free of personal neurotic difficulties. Often they simply cannot afford the necessary intensive treatment. Therefore, we must repeatedly compromise by attempting symptom removal, support on a weekly basis, or referral to groups.

Lower-class patients are sent to free clinics that have long waiting lists, to be treated by inexperienced residents who rotate in their clinic assignments, thus making it impossible for a long-term relationship to be developed. Because these decisions are only based on bare economic factors, they violate what I consider to be a basic human right — to be able to receive the best possible medical care regardless of socioeconomic status.

A second, and related idea that must be changed is the view

that because an individual has finished a training course in psychiatry, social work, or psychology, he is *ipso facto* a psychotherapist. At present the public is at the mercy of inadequate and untrained psychotherapists who unfortunately do not hesitate at times to tackle very complex problems with harmful (and sometimes lethal) results. Psychotherapy has now developed enough as a discipline so that it can be systematically taught with certification awarded for proficiency in the field.

To be in tune with one's own unconscious or the unconscious of others depends partly upon one's state of ego functioning and partly upon certain innate capacities. Professional persons with the capacity to emphathize with others and to enter into a feeling relationship with them at a deep level should be encouraged to obtain good training in psychotherapy.

Organizations such as the American Board of Psychiatry should be able to separate those who are qualified to do psychotherapy by virtue of ability, training, and experience, from those who are not. Furthermore, the Association for the Advancement of Psychotherapy and the American Academy of Psychotherapists should be urged to develop model programs and certification for qualified individuals who intend to do psychotherapy. These groups should also be responsible for sponsoring legislation to help relieve the financial burdens of those who need psychotherapy and to prevent those who are unqualified from practicing psychotherapy. Old-fashioned approaches to the education and certification of psychotherapists are no longer adequate.

In this chapter I will outline an educational curriculum for the future psychotherapist that should produce in him an optimal psychic field for his relationship with each of his patients. We can no longer assume that a few courses and some desultory supervision during a psychiatric residency are sufficient to educate a psychotherapist. Those who wish to be psychotherapists will have to familiarize themselves with a great deal of information in many other fields. I want to focus on a neglected aspect of training — one that will enable the psychotherapist to have a certain perspective on human problems and endeavors so that he can retain a sense of humility, be skeptical about various so-called schools of psychotherapy that claim to have all the answers, and recognize that many of the problems patients bring to psychotherapy have been disturbing humanity for thousands of years. The point is to make the psychotherapist aware of the various solutions to these problems that have been devised over the ages so that they can be placed into perspective. Thus, he will have more solutions at his disposal and be less inclined to think that his solutions are *the* only ones.

With respect to training psychotherapists, I agree completely with Ornstein (1968):

> The dyadic therapeutic relationship is conceived of as the primary model of the clinical psychiatrist. Knowledge of the intricacies and complexities of this relationship with all of its theoretical and therapeutic implications and unknowns is the unique tool of the psychiatrist of both today and the future. This knowledge fundamentally includes attempting to understand the major forces which have contributed to the development of the psychiatrist as well as the patient.

He points out (and I agree) that the common disappointment felt by residents in psychodynamics and their shift toward eclecticism during their training is due to pedagogic failure — from a lack of focus and perspective.

Consequently, there must be agreement on the philosophy of training and orientation reaching from the director of the program all the way down to the aides on the wards. Without such agreement, there will certainly be confusion and disappointment. Frequent meetings, formal and informal, at every level and careful selection of faculty can assure a consistent approach to psychotherapy throughout the program.

I like to distinguish between the tutor and the preceptor of a resident. The tutor works with him on various assigned tasks (case presentations, supervision, assigned readings, etc.) either individually or in a seminar. The preceptor works with him individually but informally on exchanging ideas about the training program, the philosophy of education, the resident's experiences with the tutors, and he serves as a non-threatening bridge between the resident and the faculty. The preceptor is *not* a psychotherapist for the resident but more of a friend and ombudsman; he helps the resident over the rough spots in his training and provides feedback to the faculty about what they are doing.

This curriculum is designed for the treatment of adults and adolescents (special changes would be necessary to train child therapists). It would probably be unpopular for two reasons: 1. I assume that all residency training programs in psychiatry should be divided into programs for residents who predominantly wish to do psychotherapy and programs for those who do not. This division violates tradition, but it is cruel to subject residents who do not want to become psychotherapists to the necessary intensive courses and supervision, and it is time to recognize that not all psychiatrists ought to, can, or want to do psychotherapy. 2. I assume that with careful selection, it is not necessary to have an M.D. degree to become a psychotherapist, although it is desirable. The idea of the curriculum I am presenting is to fill in the gaps in educational background. I assume that if the student can show academic proficiency in any of the curriculum subjects, he will either be excused from those courses or allowed to do advanced work.

I agree with the philosophy of education of St. John's College, Annapolis, Maryland. The goal of all courses is primarily to acquaint students with certain general principles that can be applied in understanding human behavior and the problems of the limitations of our knowledge. It is not necessary to defend any particular choice of courses or subjects; the curriculum I will outline is only to demonstrate what the educated psychotherapist ought to know.

The purpose of our educational procedures must be the "achievement of autonomy" (Booth, 1967). Such an education must begin with the homely virtue of temperance and then proceed to "the habitual effort to ask the right critical questions and to apply rigorous tests to our hunches." True education is based on the provision of leisure, defined as: "that moment which can come only to a fully conscious human being, when he is able to draw back from his activities and compare what he is doing with what

he would like to do, or could conceive as better worth doing"
(Booth, 1967).

The courses are designed to meet three hours per week, allowing three additional hours for homework, so that each course
requires a total of six hours per week. It is assumed that all students
will work a six-day week and utilize evenings for extra study when
necessary.

The most unpopular aspect of my proposal will probably be
that it leaves little time for students to do hospital chores; the
eight-hour day will be filled with either study or learning experiences. To train psychotherapists, four full years will be
necessary; since time is short, burdening residents with routine
hospital duties has no place in an honest teaching program.

Here is the outline for the program:

CURRICULUM FOR PSYCHOTHERAPISTS

(Based on an eight-hour day, six-day week, and four-
year duration.)

I. *Apprentice Work*
Hour 1: Personal psychotherapy (one or more times per week),
individual supervision, and clinical seminars.
Hours 2, 3, 4: Working with patients. In the first year: usual
hospital duties, brief therapy, somatic treatments, etc.
In second, third, and fourth years: outpatient work,
individual interests, research, etc.
II. *Theoretical Work* (all include three hours of seminar and three
hours of study per week).
Hour 5: Basic psychiatry and psychotherapy reading for four
years.
Hour 6: Practical sciences — all aspects — for four years.
Hour 7: Humanities for four years (more reading time and fewer
seminars may be necessary at certain points in this
course).

Hour 8 : Language and abstract studies. a. Two years of language (modern or classical) and the structure and evolution of language.

b. Two years of logic, mathematics, game theory, and philosophy.

I begin by dividing the eight-hour day in half. The first half would be more traditional, emphasizing technical proficiency in psychiatry and psychotherapy. One hour per day would be spent with a senior psychiatrist or psychotherapist (preferably a different one each day and rotating each year so that there would be a maximum exposure to a variety of therapists). At least one of these hours per week would be for the resident's own personal psychotherapy, which ought to be carried out over four years, and some residents will need more frequent sessions. (See the description of the Bellevue-University of Utah program, Nicklin and Branch, 1969.) The other five hours would consist of supervising the candidate's work with patients in the usual manner (see Chapter 4).

The remaining three hours of the technical proficiency half of the day would vary according to the student's interests and what is available in the individual program. In the first year of a psychiatry residency training program, for example, the usual presentation of hospitalized inpatients, somatic treatments, and basic general psychiatry would be the rule; in psychology programs, of course, the fundamentals would be somewhat different. In the second, third, and fourth years the candidate would be doing three hours of psychotherapy per day of selected patients. There should be variety in the psychotherapy experiences: Each year the student should have a greater choice of what he wants to do in psychotherapy.

Candidates should be required to attend one evening meeting per week (four per month) for the following purposes: 1. A meeting of all resident in the program by themselves to evaluate and discuss the program; 2. A meeting of all residents in the program with the director of training or chairman of the department to discuss various issues; 3. A joint scientific meeting of the faculty and students, mandatory for *all*; and 4. A journal club in which one faculty member is invited by the residents to assign readings and discuss his special area of interest and competence. These weekly meetings should be a vital part of the program.

The second half of the day would be spent in seminar or study; a tutorial system would be desirable, but most programs do not have enough well-trained teachers for that, so a seminar system must ordinarily be used. All of our knowledge is uncertain (Jones, 1969) and we need to know a great deal more about human intellectual and emotional endeavors in the past and the present before we have any right to try to enter into the lives of other human beings as an expert. An absence of this perspective and the therapist's own personality disturbances comprise the two greatest dangers to the patient.

Four hours per day for four years should be devoted to seminars and study of certain subjects, with the courses designed so that for two years six hours per week (three in seminar and three in homework) are spent on each. This will allow for eight two-year courses in four categories:

The first category (four years, one hour per day) is psychiatric and psychological literature. The classic and modern works on general psychiatry, psychology, history of psychiatry, psychodynamics, and psychotherapy can be reviewed, with a later emphasis on recent developments, research, etc. I have already presented a basic reading list for such a seminar (Chessick, 1969a), and Woods et al. (1967) have prepared a compendium of the most popular books and papers in training programs.

The second category (four years, one hour per day) may be called the practical sciences; it would consist of formal psychology, sociology, biology, anthropology, medicine, psychosomatic medicine, and the physical sciences. It *is* important for the psychotherapist to know something about the Copernican revolution and the conflicting theories about the evolution of the universe, as well as about current research in human genetics and behavior.

The third category (four years, one hour per day) would be devoted to the humanities. The student should have some knowledge of the history of art and music and then — on his own time —

acquaint himself with these fields, if he has not already done so. He should study ancient and modern literature, including biography, poetry, novels, short stories, drama, and the great classics. These works must be read carefully under seminar supervision, with emphasis on understanding human aspirations and the human condition. Finally, the candidate must have at least a basic knowledge of history (see Cantor, 1969, McNeill, 1963, and Chessick, 1968a), as well as mythology, religion, and the philosophy of history.

The fourth category is probably the most controversial, but I feel it should be mandatory. Two years, one hour per day, should be spent mastering either a modern foreign language or a classical language (Latin, Greek, Chinese, or Sanskrit). If the student has already studied a modern language, he should now study a classical language, and vice versa. The emphasis should be on understanding the structure and evolution of language and on reading some important authors in the original, especially those who lose so much in translation.

Finally, in the second half of this category (two years, one hour per day), the candidate must be introduced to what I call abstract studies — the principles of logic (both classical and modern), mathematics, and game theory. The history of philosophy should be reviewed, and the student should know about certain unsettled philosophical controversies that have an important bearing on the practice of psychotherapy and its status as a scientific discipline.

Among philosophers, Bertrand Russell became famous for his analysis of various philosophical positions, showing that they were often based on various logical or semantic mistakes. The best-known examples are from the numerous logical arguments for the existence of God, which any modern student of logic can demolish. Similarly, psychotherapists are presently being confronted with various nebulous theories with such titles as "existential psychoanalysis"; the literature is filled with high-sounding terminology, sometimes based on Greek roots and sometimes on German. Careful linguistic usage can eliminate many unintentional implications; terms and sentences should be chosen for simplicity and clarity, or else simple and clear definitions should be offered for new terms and concepts.

Psychotherapists must have a thorough understanding of their own orientation; they should be able to describe this in a clear and distinct manner and to differentiate between what they know and what they are simply not sure of. Freud was very good at this — he had the capacity to distinguish observable case material from both abstract conceptualizations and tentative concepts. A modern example of such clarity has been written by Strupp (1969).

It is not necessary that our theoretical constructions be correct, but they must be consistent, clear and accurate; and our terminology and arguments must proceed logically from them. Science makes progress when one set of theoretical constructions is replaced by another, as brilliantly described by Kühn (1962), but this cannot happen until the basic constructs are clear. The Newton of our field was Freud; whoever sets out to overturn his conceptual system must meet certain definitive criteria, but an insidious muddling of the terminology does *not* increase our knowledge. Many prominent authors are guilty of this confusion, and much of the so-called conflict between schools of psychoanalytic thought is nothing more than terminological confusion and personality conflicts.

A final and very important complaint: one must not confuse deduction and description! Describing a phenomenon in different words does *not* constitute deduction; it is nothing more than a tautology and is useful only in the second description is clearer than the first. Our terminology must not allow one to infer a pseudo-scientific authority. This is especially true in social psychiatry, where certain psychiatrists are talking about every conceivable social issue and utilizing a pseudo-scientific jargon to conceal the fact that they are just as ignorant about and frustrated with the modern world as the rest of us.

Psychotherapists can be roughly divided into two groups — the optimists and the pessimists. The extreme pessimist is typified by Freud's (1937) paper, "Analysis Terminable and Interminable." A good example of the optimistic viewpoint is presented in Wolberg's (1967) textbook, *The Technique of Psychotherapy*. Generally speaking, the pessimists believe that most emotional problems yield only bit by bit to a long psychotherapy, that a hard, nuclear infantile core must be reached in order for a therapy to succeed, that certain conservative principles of treatment are necessary to reach this infantile core (involving an intense one-to-one relationship between therapist and patient), and that the art of therapy largely consists of correctly recognizing and interpreting crucial manifestations of transference at the appropriate times. The optimists see many other factors that help to form and re-form the personality; they emphasize cultural influences and give the general impression that things are not so bad nor so difficult. They say that popularized guidebooks will help the individual (for example, "An Organized Outline for Self-Observation," in Wolberg and Kildahl, 1970). The optimists give many factors equal weight, describe all sorts of schools together, and, since there is so much disagreement, imply that almost anything goes.

Eclecticism, unless it is carefully defined, can lead one to both confusion and an insidious sense of nihilism. In other instances it can lead one to feel that psychotherapy is easy, thereby encouraging untrained or poorly trained semiprofessionals to try various innovations under the guise of therapy. Perhaps Rosenthal (1969) expressed the extreme view in claiming that "each therapist creates psychotherapy in his own image . . . . Much of what goes on in psychotherapy is preface, prologue, incidental and almost irrelevant." In this view there are no standards or correct technique — anybody can do it; psychotherapy becomes a mystical and indescribable process. The difference between the goals of psychotherapy and the goals of life becomes completely blurred and the patient does not know what to expect — only some kind of mystical experience.

From this brief discussion it ought to be clear that psychotherapists should have a substantial background in philosophy if they are to avoid various traps in their theoretical considerations and if they are to attain any real understanding of the problems of modern man. For example, Nietzsche's masterpiece *Ecce Homo: How One Becomes What One Is* (taken from the words Pilate said of Jesus [John 19:5]: "Behold the man!") tries to present a new and different image of humanity. Nietzsche struggles throughout his life and his works with the idea of man overcoming himself and developing a creative and dynamic personality so that he can look at the absurdity of human life and feel laughter and exaltation in spite of it. He recognizes the chaos of the passions and asks us to harness this chaos, but not to lose it or try to repress it as an enemy:

> I say unto you: one must still have chaos in oneself to be able to give birth to a dancing star. I say unto you: you still have chaos in yourselves [1968].

Since philosophy for psychotherapists (Hour 8 in the proposed curriculum) has been so neglected in psychiatric literature, I have devoted all of Chapter 3 to it.

With respect to the humanities course (Hour 7), a great deal of reading will be required, as well as listening to music and looking at art in the student's spare time. Besides learning about history, the development of culture, the portrayals of and suggested solutions for human problems found in classical and modern literature, the student must also learn about the possible *functions* of various art forms, including myth-making, in our attempts to solve human problems.

The significance of myth-making in psychotherapy has been presented by Ehrenwald (1966) in a somewhat extreme form. It is important for the student to realize that he cannot skillfully dissect the patient's mind on the basis of purely scientific knowledge. He should also consider that our society is heir to the Western philosophical and cultural tradition and that part of the psychotherapist's influence in his relationships with patients is by imparting the idea of civilization, that was outlined by Clark (1969). As Ehrenwald (1966) described it:

> Every individual therapist will have to do more than acquire the professional skills and experiences required by his academic curriculum. He will have to devote equal attention to acquiring the spiritual discipline, to develop the cultural awareness and the sense of values which forms the matrix of his

evolving personal myth and therapeutic presence. The gift of intuition may be one of the by-products of this development.

The study of aesthetics may help the psychiatrist to become a more sensitive human being with a greater capacity for empathy, a fact that has been almost totally overlooked in the psychiatric literature. The psychotherapist should both know about aesthetics and have experienced it personally. It seems inconceivable that a psychotherapist with no knowledge of philosophy or Western culture and with no interest in the humanities could do a successful job of intensive psychotherapy; the patient would be working with a shadow-person. In all of his work, Freud exemplified a deep understanding of culture and of the arts. To the reader who wishes to explore the need for studying the humanities, I recommend especially the views of Pater (1959), Schopenhauer (1958), Nietzsche (1968a), Tolstoy (1962), and Malraux (1953). These authors emphasize the *function* of art both as a temporary escape from life's problems and as a *direct influence upon both our intrapsychic balance and our perceptual capacities.*

The humanizing aspects of the study of philosophy, the arts, culture, and history cannot be emphasized enough. Whenever psychiatrists have shown evidence of a humane spirit, advances seem to have been made in our field; there appears to be a direct relationship between considering the individual human being as worthy of attention and the improvement of man's lot. This chapter has emphasized that in educating the psychotherapist, the goal is to produce in him an optimal psychic field. In their training, candidates will need to be relieved of many routine tasks in order to have time to study and reflect on many of the humane disciplines. A proposed curriculum has been presented that gives greater emphasis to the humanities and philosophy than ever before.

3

Philosophy for Psychotherapists

These men knew the pathos of life,
and mortal things touch their hearts.
Vergil, *Aeneid*

Truth descends only on him who tries for it, who yearns for
it, who carries within himself, pre-formed, a mental space
where the truth may eventually lodge.
Ortega y Gasset, *What Is Philosophy?*

According to Gibbon (1961), "Every man who rises above the
common level has received two educations: the first from his
teachers; the second, more personal and important, from himself."
This should be borne in mind by every psychotherapist in training,
especially as he studies philosophy and the humanities. In this
chapter I will focus on certain topics in philosophy that I believe
psychotherapists should definitely know something about. What is
philosophy? The answer is exceedingly difficult and invariably
implies a philosophical point of view (which must be subjective).
The problem is described by Nietzsche (1968a):

> What provokes one to look at all philosophers half sus-
> piciously, half mockingly, is not that one discovers again and
> again how innocent they are — how often and how easily they
> make mistakes and go astray; in short, their childishness and
> childlikeness — but that they are not honest enough in their
> work .... They all pose as if they had discovered and reached
> their real opinions through the self-development of a cold,
> pure, divinely unconcerned dialectic ... while at the bottom it
> is ... most often a desire of the heart that has been filtered
> and made abstract .... Gradually it has become clear to me
> what every great philosophy so far has been: namely, the
> personal confession of its author and a kind of involuntary
> and unconscious memoir. ...

Even though Nietzsche, in this remarkable pre-Freudian
passage, may be correct, it does not follow that all philosophy is
subjective nonsense and a waste of time. In fact, I believe that for
the psychotherapist, philosophy, carefully defined, should be a
mandatory field of study. For our purposes I would like to define
philosophy as the interminable process of uncovering the basic
assumptions behind our thinking and our behavior, and the investigation of those assumptions that cannot be tested by scientific
experiment by the use of a modified scientific method — the method
of philosophy.

Philosophy, by this definition, is the counterpart of the pyscho-
therapist's investigation of unconscious and irrational motives.
The difference is that in philosophy, no resistance is expected in
uncovering basic assumptions; if they can be proved wrong or
inferior they can readily be changed.

Let me illustrate. A man works six full days a week. He arrives
home on Saturday night shortly before he and his wife are expected
at a dinner party on her one night out; impatiently she has to wait
while he changes his shirt before they race off breathlessly. This
man's children show increasing signs of emotional disturbance as
they reach adolescence; he copes with this problem by repeating to
them again and again certain stereotyped moralizings. If this
problem were basically a philosophical one, it would not be hard
to show this man that he has confused his priorities, that his

life, which Socrates said was "not worth living" (another basic assumption), we must become familiar with philosophy.

To clarify the difference between a philosophical proposition and a psychodynamic formulation, the former refers to assumptions that we believe are true and on which we base our thinking and behavior (assumptions that cannot be validated by the method of science), and the latter refers to a set of interacting psychological forces assumed to exist within a certain individual that lead to certain behavior on his part. Whether psychodynamic formulations are "as if" hypotheses or hypotheses subject to the method of science remains a moot question (Chessick, 1961).

Since thinking persons cannot avoid philosophy, it is clear why psychotherapists must be concerned with it. However, there are additional reasons for psychotherapists to have a special knowledge of philosophy, history, and culture.

First, a knowledge of philosophy is an invaluable diagnostic and therapeutic tool. At present many patients bring up problems relating to life's absurdity and lack of meaning (Wheelis, 1958). We must be able to distinguish clearly between philosophical confusion and psychopathology. A review of the literature of both psychiatry and philosophy indicates that philosophers are often abysmally ignorant of psychiatry and mistake pyschopathology for philosophical confusion; the opposite is often true of psychiatrists. Patients presenting complaints that seem to indicate philosophical confusion should first be approached by the method of philosophy. Most of these patients will probably resist having their assumptions uncovered; even if they recognize a lack of consistency or rationality in their thinking or behavior, they probably will not change. This permits us to reach their psychopathology unless they can rationalize or intellectualize so well that other approaches are necessary. As Russell (1961) has said: "The opinions that are held with passion are always those for which no good ground exists; indeed the passion is the measure of the holder's lack of rational conviction."

Near the end of therapy patients often bring up questions that are basically philosophical and that cannot be approached by the method of science or psychotherapy. Philosophical uncertainty must not be confused with psychopathology. The identity, career line, or life style, ultimately chosen by a patient rests partly on his own philosophical assumptions. The psychotherapist may have helped the patient demolish a style of life based on neurotic unconscious motivations and philosophic chaos, but then he must permit the patient to form his own identity based on better self-knowledge and his own philosophical choices. The healthy psychotherapist can permit this without anxiety.

Second, the study of philosophy, history, and culture puts our work in perspective and affords us a sense of humbleness, thus helping us to avoid claims to rightousness and fanaticism, as emphasized by Russell (1961).[1]

> History makes one aware that there is no finality in human affairs; there is not a static perfection and an unimprovable wisdom to be achieved. Whatever wisdom we may have achieved is a small matter in comparison with what is possible. Whatever beliefs we may cherish, even those that we deem most important, are not likely to last for ever; if we imagine that they embody eternal verities, the future is likely to make a mock of us.

From this passage it should be clear why philosophy must be defined, like psychotherapy, as an *interminable* process, lasting throughout one's lifetime (Chessick, 1969b).

Third, it is obvious that in order to understand psychotherapy one must understand the philosophy of science. To gain knowledge from the psychotherapeutic process requires a philosophical study of the basic assumptions of psychiatry. The question of which aspects of psychotherapy are scientific and which are artistic is significant for both its practice and its teaching, as well as for the selection of future therapists; since this is a philosophical problem as defined

[1] Every psychotherapist should listen to the exciting and unforgettable record "Bertrand Russell Speaks" (Caedman T.C.1149).

above, it must be approached by the method of philosophy.

Finally, and perhaps most important of all, we come to the pleasure of philosophizing. It is impossible to add much to what has already been written about this from the time of Plato and Aristotle. Pursuing philosophical knowledge and applying the method of philosophy, although they promise no immediate or material gain, can make *the* vital difference in the quality of a person's life, regardless of his external circumstances.

There are two general ways that textbooks approach philosophy, besides giving a historical overview (which is rather rare). In one approach the book has a section for each of the main philosophical issues, and the author writes a continuous text in his own words summarizing the various points of view. The best examples of this I know are by Brennan (1967) and Russell (1946); others include Passmore (1957), Sprague (1961), and Joad (1946). These books are interesting because it is impossible to present an exposition of philosophy without also expressing one's own philosophical point of view; in fact, some of the greatest new works in philosophy purport to be expositions of other views of philosophical problems!

In the second approach, the text is divided by philosophical subjects and contrasting quotations of variable length are given, together with an exposition by the author or editor. Of these books I prefer Castell (1963), and Margolis (1968). Such books can be rather dull, depending on the translation chosen and the ability of the editor to put the material together coherently and meaningfully.[2]

For the psychotherapist, philosophy can be divided into ten areas:

1. *Politics and the Philosophy of History*. It is obvious that psychotherapy cannot flourish in a repressive totalitarian state —

---

[2] A third approach might also be mentioned. Some books focus on certain key philosophers, without attempting to be historically complete. An unusual and outstanding example is O'Connor (1964). Also, Copleston (1965) presents a complete review of the major philosophers from the Catholic viewpoint. These works are outstanding sources for reference.

56

one that violates privacy, insists on censorship and thought control, prohibits free discussion of issues, or makes people insecure by the use of certain police tactics. Clearly, there is a better atmosphere for psychotherapy where the individual is accorded substantial freedom and dignity. The reader is referred to Mill (Levi, 1963) and to the writings of our founding fathers for a discussion of democracy; Peterson's book on Thomas Jefferson (1970) is excellent.

It should be obvious that anyone who deals with the problems of human beings should understand political trends and have a general idea of the philosophy of history. Psychotherapists can learn much from the philosophies of history set forth by such men as Thucydides, Voltaire, Spengler, Toynbee, and others.

2. *History of Philosophy.* A really clear, straightforward book on the history of philosophy, including a discussion of the development of culture and perhaps the evolution of psychotherapy, remains to be written. Jones (1969) is probably the best, although it is difficult and thoroughly professional. The most readable books are Russell (1945) and (1959b), but they reflect his biases and are not up to date. In studying the history of philosophy, as quoted by Nietzsche earlier, there is simply no possibility of agreement on many vital philosophical issues; man is obliged to live with a degree of uncertainty about many things.

Freud pointed out that the capacity to tolerate uncertainty is an important sign of maturity. Russell said that in order to be happy, one must be able to act on principles that seem reasonable or probable, but not certain. To be paralyzed by the uncertainties of life or to react to uncertainties by withdrawal or giving up the quest for greater understanding of the problems of life is a form of intellectual impotence that often accompanies psychological disorders.

Many philosophical systems and viewpoints begin by emphasizing the uncertainty and mystery of our lives. Any psychotherapist who was unaware of the fundamental mystery of life would not be very competent since he would be out of touch with the human dilemma; any psychotherapist who subscribed *fanatically* to any political, religious, or other cause, or who thought he had *the* solutions to human problems would thereby demonstrate his ignorance of history and philosophy.

3. *The Meaning and Necessity of Philosophy.* This has been discussed earlier in this chapter.

4. *Problems of Language and Logic; Semiotic.* The obvious starting point for all philosophical study is semiotic — the general theory of signs, languages, and logic. Twentieth-century philosophers have been considerably preoccupied with these subjects; some have even attempted unsuccessfully to reduce all philosophy to linguistic problems (Lehrer, 1970). Unquestionably, many classical philosophical problems have been explained as matters of faulty logic or linguistic confusion; the problem of the existence of God is one of these. The psychotherapist should understand that philosophy has nothing to contribute to the so-called rational arguments (Mavrodes, 1970) for or against the existence of God; it can only take an agnostic position. Belief in God or any religion is strictly a matter of faith. Thus, conflict is not inevitable between philosophy and psychotherapy on the one hand, and religion on the other, except — and this is very important — when religion is used as a defense against exploring a philosophical or psychological issue. The psychotherapist cannot support the burning of philosophers at the stake for questioning religious dogma or the patient's refusal to discuss certain matters for religious reasons; he must oppose, and hopefully analyze, such attitudes.

The psychotherapist should understand logical positivism as eloquently presented by Ayer (1952, 1956), and be familiar with the basic work of Wittgenstein (1953) (believed by many to be the greatest philosopher of our century). A thorough knowledge of the pitfalls of language and logic would obviously be useful; such knowledge might help eventually to end most of the competing so-called schools of psychotherapy with their meaningless titles. At least psychotherapists should not be taken in by meretricious terminology! Anyone interested in the problems of working-through in psychotherapy should be thoroughly acquainted with the problems in semiotic and logic that I have discussed elsewhere (Chessick, 1969a).

5. *Epistemology.* Unfortunately, whoever embarks on a study of logic and semiotic will soon find himself embroiled in more difficult problems. What is truth? What is certainty? Can we really "know" anything? How do we get our knowledge of the external world? These questions are generally known as epistemology from the Greek word *episteme* (which is translated as "true knowledge"). Philosophers have written both brilliantly and foolishly on these problems.

Although there are other approaches, I believe that some sort of correspondence theory is necessary for psychotherapeutic work. We say that a given sentence is true when it corresponds to the facts, but this requires clarification. Correspondence to the facts is defined by passing certain criteria of verification. Thus, we can only say that statements are more or less certain or true — that they possess certain degrees of truth value — depending upon whether they pass our criteria of verification. Since these criteria, known as the scientific method and the philosophical method (discussed above), only represent unprovable assumptions, there can be no such thing as absolute truth or certainty (unless one wishes to define this as "ideas in the mind of God" or some such thing).

Thus, a fundamental uncertainty is built into *all* human knowledge; *episteme* is only an ideal to be approached asymptotically by repeated application of our verification procedures. Similarly, we cannot be *sure* of anything about the external world — the *noumena,* or things-in-themselves. This, of course, was suggested by Kant, who defined our notions of causality, substance, and so forth as based on "categories" of the understanding. Most post-Kantian philosophy represents either a wild attempt to build world systems about the unknowable, leading to all sorts of egregious nonsense that simply reflects the wishes of the philosopher (for example, to justify the Prussian dictatorial state) or to a withdrawal into the study of logic and semiotic as the only true business of philosophy.

6. *Philosophy of Science.* Since scientists have a different temperament, they have gone ahead blithely to change the world regardless of the ruminations of philosophers. From their spectacularly successful method arises a basic operational solution to epistemological problems. One could easily argue that philosophy of science

was a branch of epistemology, but it deserves special attention. Philosophy of science deals with the method of science and its limitations; I have tried to set forth a parallel but less dependable method for philosophy. Since the method of science has worked so well in dealing with certain problems, we could hope that a modification of this method would apply to a larger range of problems. In fact, the only other method is intuition or faith, which is impossible to discuss, extremely individualized, uncommunicable, and therefore generally useless.

Important physical scientists of our time have devised a reasonable approach to epistemology (Frank, 1947; Einstein and Infeld, 1938; and Born, 1968). One could justifiably call it a common-sense approach since these scientists posit a correlation between the external world and the perceived world, although the correlation may be distant and have many intermediate steps. Furthermore, they posit a continuity of causal lines and a correspondence of structure between the external world and our perceptions; thus, more is involved than the mind simply putting objects into the picture. Einstein calls this epistemological view an optimistic and realistic one.

The relation between scientific concepts and the external world is significant for psychotherapists since we frequently deal with these concepts. A knowledge of the scientific method and its limitations would obviate so many controversies in our field; our literature is replete with statements that even the most elementary knowledge of philosophy would enable the reader to laugh at!

Unfortunately, philosophy can be difficult and require considerable time and application to master. Since there are differences of opinion and some issues simply cannot be answered at this time, the reader who is looking for simple, easy, and practical solutions will be discouraged. One who is not familiar with these issues can easily be fooled by the most outrageous misconceptions that are presented in scientific-sounding terminology — an especially acute problem in psychotherapy.

7. *Metaphysics*. The areas of philosophy discussed so far have at least some parallel with the scientific training received by psychotherapists. In the remaining areas, we encounter problems with no

parallel in the scientific world; thus, they may appear mysterious, hard to understand, and difficult to discuss. Since metaphysics is undoubtedly the most difficult and controversial area in philosophy, it stimulates the most repulsion and disgust among "practical" men and scientists.

What is metaphysics and does it have any meaning? Although there is no agreement, even among the best philosophers of our time, the subject has intruded itself on psychotherapy (whether we like it or not) in the form of so-called existential psychotherapy; this is based on a difficult and obscure metaphysical approach — technically, Heidegger's modification of Husserl's phenomenology. However, without a substantial background in philosophy, the reader may not be able to assess statements about existentialism made by persons who claim to understand Heidegger. Dubious statements are also made on behalf of other metaphysical systems. Gilbert and Sullivan have a marvelous song about young men trying to make an impression by dropping transcendental terms everywhere! The profusion of such nonsense has given metaphysics a bad reputation.

Any attempt at change must begin with this fact: the human mind has a need to ask questions, systematize information, and construct answers — although they may turn out to be ridiculous. To argue that metaphysics is nonsense or "mental masturbation" is not going to put an end to metaphysics.

Second, metaphysics can be a very very exciting subject; I think that the only other subject capable of generating an equal or analogous type of excitement is cosmogony, purportedly a more scientific but difficult subject. (The reader is invited to think about the relationship between cosmogony and cosmology.) If a careful study of metaphysics does not generate a certain intellectual excitement in the reader, that is not necessarily the fault of metaphysics.

Third, metaphysics might be defined as cosmology and ontology — at least for the newcomer to the field. Cosmology deals with the relationship of the sciences to each other, organizing and putting into perspective the data of the various sciences in order to try to achieve a more inclusive world picture. If the sciences are represented by the blind men feeling various parts of the elephant, then cosmology is represented by an attempt to integrate their information and achieve a better picture of the elephant — hopefully one that has more truth value. This aspect of metaphysics, although controversial, is not difficult to understand.

Ontology (the study of Being), however, is much more difficult. I believe ontology has something to offer psychotherapists, both personally and in their work. What is most vital to all of us is our being-in-the-world, our intuitive sense of being alive here-and-now. This phenomenon is *unique* in that it is both the most immediate of all our convictions and the most mysterious and frightening. As Pascal (1958) wrote:

> When I consider the short duration of my life, swallowed up in the eternity before and after, the little space which I fill, and even can see, engulfed in the infinite immensity of spaces of which I am ignorant, and which know me not, I am frightened, and am astonished at being here rather than there; for there is no reason why here rather than there, why now rather than then. . . . The eternal silence of these infinite spaces frightens me.

This was the takeoff point for Heidegger and many others who followed him, but they soon become lost in clouds of turgid terminology.

Ontology (the study of Being), however, is much more difficult. Although Heidegger is an exceptionally poor model both as a human being and as an author, some of his ideas have lasting value. Unfortunately, many schools of philosophical thought and of psychotherapy claim to utilize Heidegger's ontology, but they scarcely seem to understand what he is talking about. Furthermore, although many philosophers such as Augustine, Pascal, and Nietzsche have devoted considerable attention to man's being-in-the-world, the entire matter must be scrutinized more carefully now that traditional values are breaking down and man is becoming more aware of his alone-ness. A sufficient vocabulary for communication should be formulated; in this area I agree with Ayer that Heidegger has failed.

The psychotherapist should familiarize himself with the basic existentialist writings of such authors as Kierkegaard, Nietzsche, Buber, Camus, Sartre, and Heidegger at least for the purpose of discovering how distorted and confused their ideas have become in so-called existentialist psychotherapy or, even worse, existential psychoanalysis. Some of these authors' ideas are worthy of considerable attention by the psychotherapist, especially as he gets older.

8. *The Mind-Body Problem.* This classical philosophical problem is — in a sense — part of metaphysics because it is based on the intuitive immediacy of our own mental processes, which are not understood. The psychotherapist, like everyone else, must confront the basic mystery and tragedy of life. At present there are two generally held views on the mind-body problem: the approach of materialism and that of Ryle (1949).

Materialism as simply outlined has three propositions: 1. All things and events (including mind) are the result of the behavior of physical matter or energy. 2. Whatever happens can be explained in terms of physical laws. 3. No supernatural being is required to explain the existence and nature of the world. It is easy to show that a position of mechanistic determinism does *not* follow from these propositions, and the issue of free will versus determinism remains more of a linguistic problem than anything else (see Dworkin, 1970).

According to the materialist viewpoint, mind and life are simply the consequence of physicochemical events, relentless and without purpose. There are varying degrees of strict materialism, sometimes divided into "tough-minded" and "tender-minded"; the latter, which is referred to as naturalism, represents something of a compromise between materialism and idealism.

Ryle (1949) is a landmark work on the mind-body problem that deserves careful study by all psychotherapists. He points out that the mind-body problem is an essential human mystery that cannot be solved by reducing all our conceptions to materialism. The idea of mind is a ghost concept and cannot be compared with body in any sense. Such a comparison would be like the tourist who, having been shown the buildings on a university campus, asked:

"Now show me the university!" Or it might be like trying to equate team spirit with the kickoff. The words "mind," "university," and "team spirit" represent ghost concepts. Ryle proceeds by trying essentially to eliminate mind, thereby developing a springboard to philosophical behaviorism. An outstanding review and criticism of Ryle that is especially pertinent for psychotherapists is Russell (1959a).

I am inclined to accept the materialist view of mind, but I agree with Ryle that at least *my* mind and *my* being-here-and-now-in-the-world are the ultimate mystery of *my* existence; the fact that I will inevitably cease to be represents a mysterious tragedy to me. This is a problem that everyone must face. It may be clear now that philosophical gloom can best be dispelled by successful inter-personal relations, a fact poorly understood by most philosophers, with the notable exception of Hume. In *Anna Karenina*, Tolstoy presented an autobiographical passage on the enigma of death, a matter that preoccupied him most of his life:

> The sight of his brother and the nearness of death revived in Levin that sense of horror in the face of the insoluble enigma, together with the nearness and inevitability of death . . . even less than before did he feel capable of apprehending the meaning of death, and its inevitability rose up before him more terrible than ever . . . . But now, thanks to his wife's presence, that feeling did not reduce him to despair. In spite of death, he felt the need for life and love. He felt that love saved him from despair, and that this love, under the threat of despair, had become stronger and purer. The one mystery of death, still unsolved, had scarcely passed before his eyes, when another mystery had arisen, as insoluble, calling to love and to life.

9. *Ethics.* Broadly speaking, this subject encompasses two basic questions: What is right, or moral? and What is a good or happy life? Some philosophers, notably Kant, have considered these two questions as identical, but for the most part they are treated

separately. Concepts of morality have changed substantially in our century; there is no absolute standard of morals now except the principle of "Do unto others as you would have them do unto you" or the ten commandments. In a formal sense that which is moral can be defined only in terms of what is socially useful, altruistic, and producing maximum happiness for all; it requires use of the philosophical method. Although this concept of morality is rather unsatisfactory, it is the best available. It must be emphasized that only *acts* or *behavior* have a moral connotation, not thoughts, feelings, or fantasies. Acts that contribute to general human welfare may be called morally good; those that diminish it are bad. In this sense, therefore, most human behavior is neither especially good nor bad.

It is difficult to assess morality because of the problem of motivation. Psychiatry has demonstrated that there is no such thing as a pure or completely altruistic motive; all human behavior has multiple determinants. Should behavior that improves human welfare but is performed largely because of selfish motives be called "moral"? If a man invents a product that will reduce air pollution and markets it in the hope of making a fortune, is this moral behavior?

One approach to this question is to call all moral judgments essentially emotional expressions of whether or not we *feel* an act is good. By reducing the issue of morality to semantics, we have a rather extreme viewpoint. In my opinion, two other approaches would be much more useful: 1. Any doctrine that arbitrarily sets what is right (aside from the golden rule and the ten commandments) is very dangerous and could easily be subverted into an excuse for an *auto-da-fé*, which humans love so much. 2. The distinction between "morally good" and "I approve" must remain fuzzy and subject only to analysis by philosophical method. Thus, behavior should be judged by both motive and consequence; it can be placed on a continuum ranging from a bad act with evil motive and bad consequences at one end to a good act with altruistic motive and good consequences at the other end. With this scheme it would be easy to classify some behavior (for example, that of Hitler) and very difficult to classify other behavior (for example, that of President Lyndon Johnson). Brody (1970) and Gauthier (1970) offer worthwhile reading on this matter.

Freud pointed out that happiness should be related to pleasure, or at least to the release of dammed up tensions. Thus, he saw happiness as a temporary phenomenon that depends upon the intensity of the release. Pleasure can generally be conceived of as brief and intense or prolonged and not so intense. Furthermore, since there are pleasures of both the mind and the body, gratification of both can bring a sense of happiness, or at least contentment (*ataraxia*). There is little agreement on the exact meaning of "pleasure" or on the relationship between happiness to contentment.

Pleasures of the body include sexual gratification as well as satisfaction of the need for sleep, food, drink, shelter, and warmth. They also include a sense of physical security and freedom from disease. These pleasures overlap with those of the mind, which include friendships with others; communion with nature; the enjoyment of art, music, and literature; study and contemplation; and possibly even certain types of games and play.

It is clear that the happiest life would probably include many pleasures of both types; any other concept of happiness would be a distortion of the term. People who are able to cultivate the pleasures of the mind have an advantage over those who do not, for they depend less on their physical environment for a sense of contentment; they also have an additional means for enjoying life, which is fraught with what Freud called "everyday misery."

Nietzsche spoke of the presence of an Apollonian and Dionysian principle in all human mentation (1968a). The Apollonian represents the need for control, order, understanding — the rational; the Dionysian represents the seething cauldron of human emotions. In order to achieve a good or happy life, some kind of integration of these forces is necessary, but this is extremely difficult to accomplish because the forces are powerful and often opposed. Is it any wonder the Buddha wrote, "He who conquers himself is the greatest of all conquerors"? The lives of most people are full of perpetual and unexamined chaos; therefore, they are easily swayed by demagogues who offer simplistic solutions to life's problems and a chance to commit violence.

10. *Aesthetics.* This is the study of the general principles of the creation and appreciation of art, including all art forms. The first problem is to establish a division among the arts, a difficult task because present-day artists like to experiment in many directions. The second problem is to define art itself: What is beauty? What is aesthetic excellence? The psychotherapist may wonder what bearing aesthetics has on psychotherapy. Its relevance emerges when we attempt to define aesthetic excellence, for then we arrive at the general matter of creativity and the motives behind it.

Freud viewed art as a projection of the artist's psyche, which could be psychoanalyzed like a dream. Schopenhauer (1958) stressed the escape aspect of art, a temporary release from the striving of the Will; he said that one could achieve temporary contentment by immersing oneself in art. Nietzsche, on the other hand, emphasized the exciting and refining aspects of art for the human psyche. Similarly, Pater (1959) said that art gives quality to our brief life, not calm, and that it helps to expand the interval of our life by "as many pulsations as possible." Malraux (1953) saw all of art as a revolt against man's tragic fate. It would appear that a human life devoid of the arts is missing something vital.

In psychotherapy literature there is little recognition of the importance of immersing oneself in art, although there are many papers on the metapsychology of creativity. Art has many vital functions that an individual can use as needed, and there are many kinds of art and many media and sensory modalities through which it can be experienced. All appreciation of beauty is a temporary escape from everyday problems; art can even permit an individual to revolt if he wishes. Art can take a person temporarily outside of himself, enabling him to merge himself spiritually with the cultural achievements of others. If art allows one to escape temporarily, calms one, excites and refines one, or improves one, it can be called beautiful; thus, we are defining beauty in terms of its capacity to produce certain effects. By this definition many things partake of beauty, which is, after all, primarily an intuitive conviction about the effect of a given experience. As a pleasure of the mind, aesthetic appreciation is closely related to happiness, and both are important in assessing the quality of a person's life.

My discussion of these ten areas of philosophy is only intended to be a starting point for the reader's own thinking and exploration and to illustrate the importance of philosophy for psychotherapists. Philosophizing, like personal psychotherapy, must be a lifetime process; if I have succeeded in convincing the reader of this, I have accomplished my major aim here.

I should like to present a *minimum* reading list in philosophy that ought to be required in the training of every psychotherapist. This list does *not* represent a course in philosophy, nor is it in any sense inclusive. The books have been chosen primarily because of their importance for psychotherapists and secondarily to introduce the psychotherapist to certain philosophers and their methods of approach. Only those philosophers who deal with important issues for today have been included. (Those who have primarily utilized a mystical or religious approach have been omitted, except St. Augustine, who offers a great deal for the psychotherapist to think about.)

These works should be read in the best possible translations (I have sometimes indicated my preference). Readings marked with an asterisk (*) are especially difficult and should preferably be undertaken in a seminar. These works are listed in preferred order of reading; most of them are readily available, many in paperback editions. This outline has been designed for a two-year seminar (Hour 8).

ETHICS

1. Plato (1937, trans. Jowett): *Dialogues:* Protagoras, Phaedo, Symposium, Apology, Philebus (if time, *The Republic**)[3]
2. Aristotle (1941, trans. McKeon): *Nichomachean Ethics**[4]
3. Aurelius (Staniforth, 1964): *Meditations* (if time, Epicurus [Oates, 1940]: *Fragments* and Epictetus [Oates, 1940]: *Discourses*)
4. Augustine (1951): *Confessions*
5. Spinoza (Runes, 1957): *Ethics**
6. Voltaire (1949): *Candide,* and other selections

7. Mill (1960): *Autobiography* and Levi, A. (1963): *The Six Great Humanistic Essays of John Stuart Mill*
8. Russell, B. (1968): *The Conquest of Happiness* (if time, *Basic Writings* [1961])
9. James, W. (1967): *Essays on Faith and Morals*
10. Kierkegaard (1954): *Fear and Trembling** and *Sickness Unto Death**
11. Nietzsche (1968b, ed. Kaufmann): *Thus Spoke Zarathustra** (if time, *Basic Writings** [1968a, ed. Kaufmann])
12. Camus (1957): *The Stranger* (if time, Sartre [1964]: *Nausea*)

EPISTEMOLOGY AND METAPHYSICS

1. Russell (1946): *The Problems of Philosophy*
2. Brennan (1967): *The Meaning of Philosophy*
3. Landesman (1970): *The Foundations of Knowledge* and Born (1968): "Symbol and Reality" (in *My Life and My Views*)
4. Locke (Burtt, 1939): *An Essay Concerning Human Understanding*
5. Hume (Burtt, 1939): *An Enquiry Concerning Human Understanding*
6. Kant (1963): *Critique of Pure Reason**[5]
7. Ayer (1952): *Language, Truth and Logic* (if time, Ayer [1956]: *The Problems of Knowledge*)
8. Wittgenstein (1953): *Philosophical Investigations**
9. Langer (1951): *Philosophy in a New Key*
10. Collingwood (1967): *An Autobiography*
11. Ortega y Gasset (1960): *What Is Philosophy?*
12. Heidegger (1962): *Being and Time**[6]

---

[3] For assistance, see Shorrey (1965) and Crombie (1962).

[4] For assistance, see Allan (1952) and Ross (1963).

[5] For assistance, see Jones (1969) and Ewing (1967). An easier approach is *An Immanuel Kant Reader* (Blakney, 1960).

[6] For assistance, see Schmitt (1969) and Gelven (1970). A more advanced discussion may be found in Naess (1968) and Brock (1968). An outstanding book on Heidegger is Grene (1957).

PHILOSOPHY OF SCIENCE AND THE MIND-BODY PROBLEM

1. Lucretius (Oates, 1940): *On the Nature of Things*
2. Einstein and Infeld (1938): *Evolution of Physics* and Frank, P. (1947): *Einstein: His Life and Times*
3. Schaffer, J. (1968): *Philosophy of Mind*
4. Descartes (1945, trans. Veitch): *Meditations*
5. Bernard (1949): *An Introduction to the Study of Experimental Medicine* (Part One)
6. Freud (1925): *Negation,* and "Kris: Nature and Validation of Psychoanalytic Propositions," reprinted in *Readings in Philosophy of Science* (Wiener, 1953) (if time, this entire volume is excellent)
7. Ryle, G. (1949): *The Concept of Mind**
8. Sullivan, J. (1952): *The Limitations of Science*
9. Popper (1965): *Conjectures and Refutations**
10. Russell (1948): *Human Knowledge**
11. Kuhn (1962): *The Structure of Scientific Revolutions*
12. Adler (1965): *The Conditions of Philosophy*

OUTSTANDING ADVANCED READING AND REFERENCE

1. Levi, A. (1959): *Philosophy and the Modern World*
2. Jones, W. T. (1969): *History of Western Philosophy*
3. Fleming, W. (1968): *Arts and Ideas*
4. McNeill, W. (1963): *The Rise of the West*
5. *Encyclopaedia of Philosophy* (Edwards, 1967)

This chapter defined philosophy as a never-ending process of uncovering the basic assumptions of our thinking and behavior, and an investigation by the use of the method of philosophy of assumptions that cannot be tested by scientific experiment. This method requires that our basic assumptions be logically consistent with each other and presented with a minimum of undefined terms. This method then tests our assumptions against the common experience of mankind, the historical process, and the consequences of other situations in which the same assumptions prevailed.

each role is used according to the requirements of a given situation. My own view is that the resident's anxiety level ought to determine the extent to which the supervisor should be didactic and the extent to which he should try to approach the resident's unconscious processes that are interfering with his patient work. Thus, supervisory maneuvers will depend upon the resident's anxiety level.

This view is analogous to the one set forth in Chessick (1969a), in which I urge the therapist to take the patient as far toward uncovering and self-understanding as he is able to go, using the patient's anxiety level as a gauge of what he can tolerate. Thus, therapy is tailored to fit the patient rather than trying to fit the patient into the therapist's preconceived idea of what therapy should be. Similarly, it is preferable for the supervisor to shift from didactic to uncovering techniques, depending upon his evaluation of the resident's ego and current anxiety level. The remainder of this chapter will discuss questions that must be raised before supervision can be considered a scientific process.

What does the resident yearn for? One must always keep in mind what Emch (1955) calls "the social context of supervision." The student hopes to receive from the supervisor "potent remedies" — both realistic and magical — in order to increase his sense of power and competence. He also wants to please his supervisor, to make impressive presentations in seminars in order to achieve prestige among his peers, and to have his work accredited by the training program. These hopes compete and sometimes interfere with what ought to be his primary wish: "to be an effective therapist with his patient for the patient's sake." An extremely complicated and disruptive situation can occur when social pressures on the resident arising from his own yearnings are contradicted by the supervisor's goals for him. For example, if the institution is primarily oriented toward preparing administrative psychiatrists while the supervisor is pressuring the resident to spend a lot of time doing intensive individual therapy, a conflict will invariably arise in the resident.

The resident is also under severe personal pressures. Because of his feeling of emptiness resulting from the three problems mentioned earlier, the resident is looking for "a magical figure in a fantasy of future omnipotence." He looks to the supervisor either for omniscience or omnisentience, as described by Sharaf and Levinson (1964). In his yearning for magical power, the resident will inevitably be disappointed; this disappointment will be extremely intense if the supervisor pretends to have such power or if he has not worked through such yearnings in his own psyche. It may come as a shock for the resident to discover that even if he slavishly imitates the supervisor, his patients do not get well.

Certain assumptions underlying supervision should be carefully scrutinized. For example, can the resident accomplish a substantial change in his work ego under supervision without simultaneously changing his personal self in psychotherapy? What is the relationship between the ego systems that comprise the work ego and those that comprise the personal self?

What does the supervisor expect and why does he supervise? Although few answers are offered in the literature, it is obvious that these questions must be dealt with, for if the needs of the supervisor are not met, he will undoubtedly do a poor job and surely disappoint the resident. From the supervisory process the supervisor derives both primary and secondary gains. The primary gains arise from the fact that he is devoting himself to the personality growth of others, is generally respectful and trustworthy, and is neither exploitative nor retaliatory. His devotion to personality growth is generally transmitted to the new psychotherapist, who may in turn want to teach and help prepare future psychotherapists. As Ekstein and Wallerstein (1958) maintain:

Teachers should get their deepest gratification not from the fact that their point of view prevails, but rather that they have developed methods of teaching which insure growth in knowledge and guarantee collaborators who stimulate them to test and to further develop their scientific assumptions. The best teachers will be eternal learners, and as such they will help their students to identify with their activity and their own process of constant growth, rather than with static opinions that become frozen dogmas of limited usefulness.

In my opinion these primary gains, laudatory as they may be, are not really sufficient to motivate most supervisors. There must be other gains; these are not pleasant to talk about because they appeal to the less noble, sublime, and mature aspects of the supervisor's personality. But, since they have a practical importance, ignoring them would be like one's failure to see hazards underfoot while walking along gazing at the stars.

The secondary gains include professional companionship for the psychotherapist who is isolated in his office, a chance to discuss his ideas and expose himself to the criticism of intelligent residents, an opportunity to rethink his basic assumptions and to review the literature, the holding of a teaching appointment which has competitive value, and whatever narcissistic gratification may be obtained by being a faculty member alongside one's former teachers and by having a voice in the accreditation of future colleagues.

Disappointment in the resident-supervisor relationship is analogous to failure in psychotherapy. When the needs of either the resident or the supervisor are not being met, communicated, or worked through, the result will be failure and disappointment. I shall try to give a few examples of this. Tischler (1968) presents a number of rather amusing reports of the resident's perception of his initial supervisory experience, similar to the one described at the beginning of this chapter. These reports all indicate a confusion of goals between the resident and the supervisor. If there is a conflict in psychotherapy between what the patient is looking for and what the therapist is attempting to do, failure is inevitable unless the matter is brought to the surface and resolved. In training, the supervisor must recognize that the resident may have goals that differ from his own and be willing to help the resident expose and discuss his goals.

An example presented by Allen et al. (1958) might be described as taking too much for granted. They report that supervisors sometimes assume at the outset that the residents know certain technical matters and fundamentals of therapy that they do not know. The residents then pretend to have the knowledge in order to save face. Anyone who has overheard the conversation of residents or a developed a good supervisory alliance will know that there is a great deal of face-saving. If the supervisor does not recognize what the resident needs because of some lack of empathy, the resident, who is subject to various pressures, will try to hide his needs — even if this means he learns nothing from his supervisor. As Semrad (1969) pointed out, being supervised is painful for every resident; it is almost like a narcissistic injury —

one in which his ideal image of himself as possessor of a personality with penetrating insightfulness and curative power is badly shaken. There follows the threat or actual occurrence of anxiety and a lowering of self-esteem which is felt as depression.

Since the supervisor is "an ambivalent object of painful growth" to the resident, he will have to face serious hostility periodically from the resident because of transference phenomena and the narcissistic wound he inflicts on the resident as part of the supervisory process. Grotjahn (1955) points out that in many ways it is more difficult to face the hostility of one's future colleagues than the hostility of one's patients, and I, too, have found this to be true; this matter does not seem to be discussed in sufficient detail in the literature.

Many residents complain that supervisors have overloaded schedules, "no time," or are poorly prepared, which may indicate that some supervisors are avoiding intense interpersonal experiences with residents by a variety of minor acting-out procedures. It is possible that the prolonged bombardment of the supervisor by the ambivalent emotions of residents over the years will (unless special precautions are taken) first lead to a feeling of boredom (which, of course, masks anxiety) and eventually to a loss of the desire to teach. Just as the resident may lose his desire to learn because of a failure in the supervisory alliance (which is manifested by coming late to sessions or forgetting sessions), the supervisor may act out in the same way.

How can we avoid disappointment in the resident-supervisor relationship? I would like to make ten concrete proposals for setting up a training program that would obviate such disappointment:

1. The conflict between the hospital's need for as many hands as possible and the development of a good teaching program must be resolved. There is a tendency for hospitals to accept almost anyone who applies for the psychiatric training program in order to fill its many service needs. But a good training program requires the careful selection of both residents and supervisors. The training committee may have to renounce its wish for a supervisor who has a famous name but is a poor supervisor in practice or renounce the residency applications of many physicians who could easily fulfill the hospital's service needs but who do not have the capacity to develop psychological-mindedness. Such renunciations would be very difficult, considering the current pressures felt by hospitals and training programs.

2. More seminars are necessary for the purpose of studying the humanities, literature, philosophy, drama, and other aspects of human experience. Seminars should be carefully coordinated and reading lists should be exchanged so that supervisors and seminar leaders may refer to the books and papers that the residents have presumably read. Seminars should be under continuous evaluation by both the residents and the training committee.

3. A good training program should include a regular seminar for supervisors. Effective supervision is extremely difficult; there are many unsolved problems in the supervisory process; and there are serious responsibilities in training new psychiatrists. A seminar for supervisors would permit and encourage the exchange of information and experiences among them as well as contribute to their growth.

4. How can we motivate supervisors who are busy in private practice to get together? It is not easy. Escoll and Wood (1967), for example, tried to ease this problem and foster cohesion in the group "by scheduling monthly dinner meetings of all preceptors to discuss matters of mutual interest," but the outside supervisors did not come regularly. It must be made clear to the outside supervisor

what the demands of the program are and what his role will be, or the program should not use outside supervisors at all. It is reasonable to expect that if outside supervisors understand the problems of supervision and if the training program is meeting *their* needs, they will respond to reasonable demands.

5. Tischler (1968) and others have suggested using a preceptor system. Each resident would be assigned to a preceptor who would function not as a supervisor but as the "resident's man," bringing the resident's problems with his seminars and his supervisors to the attention of the training committee. Similarly, the training program should encourage the formation of a residents' organization, enabling them to speak to the training committee as a group. This would facilitate honest communication since no individual would be held responsible for criticisms expressed.

6. Every effort should be made to utilize the supervisor in those capacities that interest him the most and for which he is best qualified. Care should be taken to assign supervisors to the type of residents with which they are most effective. Rosenbaum (1963) suggests, for example, that a beginning resident might feel more comfortable and gain greater emotional support from a warm, kindly, benevolent, and nonthreatening supervisor, whereas an advanced resident might be bored with him. Furthermore, all supervisors should be personally involved in their role as preceptor and in the selection and continuous evaluation of residents. Fleming and Benedek (1966) discuss the kind of evaluative function and reports that a supervisor might provide to help the training committee.

7. The training program should help to develop an *esprit de corps* among the staff so that the graduates will want to return as supervisors in order to maintain their association with the institution. Although the creation and maintenance of such an *esprit de corps* is an art, it requires open communication among residents, supervisors, and administrators and frequent social contact and informal meetings of all members of the group.

8. In addition to periodic evaluations of the resident by the supervisor, there should be periodic evaluations of the supervisor by the resident. Such evaluations would provide important data for

both the training committee and the supervisor; it follows that the length of time during which each resident is supervised by a specific supervisor should be variable. Therefore, no rigid rules should be allowed to interfere with the supervisory process and the consequent growth and development of the resident.

9. The training committee should realize that no one except a genius could possibly become an adequate psychotherapist without personal psychotherapy. This is not to imply that every resident should undergo a prolonged psychoanalysis, but fairly early in his residency he should be sufficiently motivated to try to secure some kind of psychotherapeutic help. If by the second year of his training, the resident does not strongly feel the need for personal psychotherapy, there has either been a mistake in selecting him or a pedagogic failure. The task of the training committee is to provide an atmosphere in which residents in psychotherapy are comfortable and do not feel inferior to their colleagues, and to help the residents (via the preceptor) contact effective psychotherapists in the community. It goes without saying that no supervisor, preceptor, or administrator in the program who is in contact with the residents should simultanously be giving them psychotherapy.

10. Last but not least, a supervisor's secondary gains must be carefully considered. He should receive maximum financial remuneration and have an adequate opportunity for friendly meetings with colleagues through regularly scheduled meetings. Every effort should be made to arrange supervision and seminar time to suit the convenience of the supervisor. In the case of outside supervisors, all time conflicts among staff meetings, administrative conferences, and supervisory responsibilities should be resolved in their favor. Supervisors deserve titles and perhaps even different levels of titles to work toward (for example, instructor, attending supervisor, or senior supervisor). The training committee should make certain that the university appointments of supervisors are protected and that regular promotions in rank are provided. The training committee may want to recommend the promotion of supervisors who have made outstanding contributions. It could use awards, meritorious mentions, and assignment to various panels and committees in the local

psychiatric society as recognition for a supervisor's devoted contribution. Thus, every effort must be made to provide for the supervisor's needs, while making demands on him, in order to minimize disappointments in the resident-supervisor relationship.

The second generally accepted way of teaching psychotherapy is by use of the seminar. This technique has many serious defects and has been extensively criticized in recent years. Halmos (1966) speaks about the paradox of the "faith in shortcuts and expediencies." The psychoanalytically oriented teacher recognizes that intellectual insight and direct didactic instruction are very poor methods for bringing about changes in people. Yet our seminars all assume that such didactic instruction, largely spoon-fed, will change the professional self of the resident. Here is an interesting, unexplored area for research. Ekstein and Wallerstein (1958) point out that teaching methods based on information-giving — "the authoritative transmission of technical advice" — may actually be detrimental since they tend to reflect the supervisor's way of doing things rather than to evoke the professional self of the student.

One of the few studies available of a less authoritative type of seminar, the so-called continuous case conference, carried out by Guiora et al. (1967), indicates that it is a total failure as a learning experience. Guiora's report may be too pessimistic, but perhaps other types of seminars have not been sufficiently explored. A more serious objection to any seminar on psychotherapy arises from the question of whether a process such as psychotherapy, which is only in part intellectual, can be studied intellectually without losing sight of certain really important aspects. Unfortunately, anyone who tries to teach psychotherapy, whether by individual supervision or by seminar, is setting out on almost totally uncharted waters with little but instinct to guide him. This is another aspect of the "faith of the counsellors," described by Halmos (1966). It is a pity that many teachers seem to follow the ironic precept of Galbraith (1958): "It is a far, far better thing to have a firm anchor in nonsense than to put out on the troubled seas of thought."

There are certain advantages to the seminar method of teaching psychotherapy that would justify continuing it. If we could be aware of these advantages as well as the problems faced by residents, perhaps we could design a seminar to maximize the advantages and help with the problems. The advantages of the seminar method pertain mainly to the resident's problem of identification with his instructors, his commitment to dynamic psychiatry, and his identity as a psychiatrist doing psychotherapy (many residents never develop such an identity).

The skilled seminar leader takes advantage of the fact that a seminar is like a class (which the resident has been accustomed to) and that there is safety in numbers. Thus there should be less interpersonal anxiety, except perhaps when the resident is presenting a case. Obviously the skilled seminar leader must exert pressure to prevent the seminar members from tormenting the resident who is presenting a case; such tormenting can be accounted for by many factors in both individual and group dynamics. The seminar leader must emphasize the alliance of the group and the use of case presentations as a teaching experience; these recommendations are analogous to those of Greenson (1965) for maintaining the therapeutic alliance. In the seminar there is less pressure to identify and there is less of an anxiety-driven tendency to introject the seminar leader, except for the most disturbed residents who are already overwhelmed with anxiety. The seminar gives the resident a chance to look the leader over and perhaps identify with bits and pieces of him while rejecting other parts of him that are not compatible with the resident's own style.

Only the most unenlightened supervisor would expect the resident to pattern his therapeutic identity on a style alien to his own personality; the best we hope for are partial identifications and corrections which can continue if the anxiety is not overwhelming. Some residents may choose not to do any uncovering psychotherapy at all; the seminar can allow enough interpersonal distance so that the resident need not feel guilty if he does not develop an intense commitment to what his supervisor wishes him to do. Traditional seminars have tended to neglect the doubt of many residents about the efficacy of psychotherapy. (Many residents are not in psychotherapy themselves.) They may have cases for only short periods and may be expected to accept on faith the value of uncovering psychotherapy, which usually proceeds very slowly over years.

Rosenbaum (1953) points out that many residents experience more anxiety when they start psychotherapeutic work with outpatients than when they are assigned to an inpatient service. In the latter, immediate help is available when difficulties arise, and others are also responsible for the total handling of the patient. When the resident undertakes psychotherapy with outpatients, however, he is more or less on his own in a situation in which he is attempting to master therapeutic techniques that are far less structured and stereotyped than those used in an inpatient service. In fact, it is rather interesting (although painful) to watch the resident who is beginning with outpatients after an initial inpatient experience; he tends to flounder around while trying to use the same highly structured techniques such as immediate drug-giving, getting the patient to participate in simultaneous group therapy, or environmental manipulation. Most of these maneuvers, of course, reflect the resident's anxiety and can produce chaos in the patient.

To try to alleviate the residents' anxiety, I developed a prediction seminar to be presented to residents at the time they begin outpatient psychotherapy. Obviously such a seminar must be led by someone who has devoted most of his professional life to doing uncovering psychoanalytically oriented outpatient psychotherapy, or else the seminar would have no identification value. In this seminar, which tends to run about two hours (but could be divided into two one-hour sessions for each presentation, although this is less desirable), a resident presents a case that has been in psychotherapy with him for at least a month, but preferably longer. First he presents the complete diagnostic work-up in detail, as in a diagnostic case conference. Then he outlines the therapeutic plan he formed for the patient in the first few sessions, and each seminar member is called upon individually to predict what will happen in the therapy, to predict what transference manifestations will appear, and to correct the diagnostic formulation and therapeutic plan. The group also discusses the appearance and prediction of countertransference manifestations, but it must be guided carefully in order to preserve the alliance. Soon the residents are actively commenting upon and correcting each other's approaches. The presenting resident is then required to report in detail on the last few therapeutic sessions with the patient and on the progress of the therapy to date. Past predictions are either verified or negated, which leads to further study of the therapeutic process, plans, and strategy.

During the seminar I acted in such a way that the residents had an opportunity to get to know me and so attention was shifted away from the weaknesses of the presenting resident. I recounted many anecdotes about successes and failures in my own private practice (carefully disguised to preserve the privacy of my patients) when they were appropriate to the cases being discussed. I often interrupted the presenting resident (after first explaining that I would do so) to make a general principle or present a clinical "pearl" — residents are especially hungry for these — and I tried to get the group to empathize with the presenting resident. When the group members interacted, especially when they compared notes on one another's approaches or therapeutic styles, I became passive and allowed them to interact as much as possible. When the group members were anxious or attacked one another, I became active and restrained them. I allowed the group much time to ventilate their fears and anxieties about doing psychotherapy. I often presented didactic material, which sometimes served as an anxiety-reducing device. At the beginning of the seminar, we reviewed the whole process of uncovering and supportive therapy. I offered the first case presentation, for which I deliberately chose a case from my practice in which blatant therapeutic failure occurred. (One must always bear in mind the problem of the supervisor appearing to be omnipotent.)

This seminar has been tried out during the past ten years with second- and third-year residents in psychiatry at Northwestern University, Illinois State Psychiatric Institute, and the U.S. Public Health Service. Residents from each institution, of course, presented characteristic individual difficulties. The residents were asked to keep a diary in which they would record their feelings and impressions of *each* seminar session as they occurred. Some residents kept the diary and others did not. After six months to a year in the seminar, the residents were asked to complete an anonymous questionnaire, designed to learn what their reactions were and what effect the seminar had on their difficulties.

The seminar was generally received with enthusiasm, which the residents transmitted to the succeeding class, thereby facilitating its acceptance by later classes. Replies to the questionnaire illustrated the difficulty of teaching such a seminar. For example, some seminar members wanted more didactic material such as lectures and readings; others found the didactic material rather boring and unnecessary. Most residents were satisfied with the way in which the seminar leader managed the case presentations, but a few thought he was too hard on the presenting resident and a few thought he was too easy. There was almost unanimous agreement that the most boring aspect of the seminar was when residents made poorly organized case presentations. It would appear, therefore, that the seminar should be presented only after residents have learned how to work up and effectively present a psychiatric case, which ideally they should learn in the first year.

Very few residents felt that the seminar had changed their personality in any significant way, although they all said it had helped them as psychotherapists. During the seminar this had not been clear, probably because the typical beginner is preoccupied with the technical details of psychotherapy. Those who reported feelings of anxiety generally said that these feelings pertained to how and when to make interpretations.

Perhaps the most thoughtful and articulate reply to the questionnaire was received from a resident who was among the least impressive in the seminar. (This resident revealed her identity by saying that she had made the first case presentation.) She indicated clearly what residents typically experience:

I volunteered for the first case presentation to "get it over with." Before the presentation another resident said to me: "I'd like to see how he is going to tear you to pieces!" As it turned out you did not do that at all . . . . I consider it most important for an effective supervisor to recognize the limit where provocation of anxiety improves functioning and where it becomes paralyzing. Early in my residency I had a nightmarish experience with a supervisor which nearly pushed me to quitting. Today, with more training and experience I would know much better how to handle it. I have learned to set limits and say: sorry, it's more than I can deliver.

In discussing the anxieties and the problems of the resident in psychiatry, Ford (1963) points out that "the actual control mechanism of the psychiatrist's personality — his perceptual ego — is under constant probing and provocation from the anxious energy transferred by his patient." The prediction seminar is intended to help unanalyzed novices by structuring outpatient psychotherapy and enabling residents to freely discuss "the acute sense of incompetence and of an inner void" (Sharaf, 1964) they feel at the beginning of such psychotherapy. The seminar provides structure by emphasizing the scientific method and by enabling residents to hear an experienced psychotherapist tangle (not always successfully) with the same problems. The seminar also gives the resident a chance to see the possibility of predictability in psychotherapy, which will contribute to his growing commitment to psychotherapy as a meaningful and worthwhile procedure.

This chapter has dealt with the complicated resident-supervisor relationship. It was pointed out that the resident suffers from an identity crisis, from anxiety that results from learning psychodynamics, and from a lack of deep conviction about psychotherapy. Since the basic objective of the training program is to increase awareness and understanding of the dynamic unconscious and of intrapsychic conflict in the patient-therapist relationship, it is clear that the supervisor should try to facilitate increased awareness and understanding. Otherwise, the resident will be a mediocrity, narcissistically constricting his approach, and have little true understanding of any aspect of psychiatry.

The supervisor tries to help the work ego of the resident mature by identification, reduction of anxiety, widening of the resirent's personal and literary experience, didactic teaching based on clinical phenomena presented by the resident's patients, and his own relationship with the resident. These techniques are used depending upon the state of the resident's ego at a given time and a careful assessment of his anxiety level.

At present supervision is a poorly worked out procedure. The resident is under many social pressures that may conflict with the supervisor's goals. Sometimes the resident attempts to resolve his identity crisis, anxiety, and lack of conviction by a quest for omnipotence to be achieved through introjection of the supervisor. Many technical and metapsychological questions about the supervisory process remain unanswered. The impact of prolonged supervision on the supervisor and his needs have tended to be neglected. When the needs of the resident or the needs of the supervisor are not being met, communicated, or worked through, the resident and the supervisor will disappoint each other.

There are many difficulties in teaching psychotherapy by individual supervision and the seminar. Therefore, I developed the prediction seminar; responses from residents indicate that it seems to be worthwhile and merits further trial.

5

Clinical Studies of Failure in Psychotherapy

Essentially the humanness of the analyst is expressed in his compassion, his concern, and his therapeutic intent toward his patient. It matters to him how the patient fares; he is neither just an observer nor a research worker. He is a physician and a therapist, a treater of the sick and suffering, and his aim is to help the patient get well. However, the "medicine" he prescribes is insight, carefully regulating the dosage, keeping his eye on the long-range goal, sacrificing temporary and quick results for later and lasting changes. The humanness is also expressed in the attitude that the patient has rights and is to be respected as an individual. He is to be treated with ordinary courtesy; rudeness has no place in psychoanalytic therapy. If we want the patient to work with us as a co-worker on the regressive material that he produces, we must take care that the mature aspects of the patient are consistently nurtured in the course of our analytic work.

R. Greenson,
The Technique and Practice of Psychoanalysis

This chapter is based on a careful review of all patients encountered in the author's private practice of outpatient psychoanalytically oriented psychotherapy during the past ten years. I want to discuss failure in psychotherapy from the therapist's point of view, without referring to pertinent factors in the patient (these have been discussed by — among others — Hoch, 1948, and Anna Freud, 1969). Sitting in the psychotherapist's chair, I invite the reader to stand behind me and look over my shoulder in order to discover what the psychotherapist in practice encounters. Such an approach is bound to emphasize the therapist's weaknesses; even if he is doing a proper job, it is clear that many problems will arise out of the very nature of the psychotherapeutic situation — in many ways a unique encounter.

All patients I met in my practice can be divided into four general categories. First there were patients whom I saw for one, two, or three interviews for diagnostic purposes *only,* where it had been agreed in advance that *no* recommendations would be made for treatment. This group included patients who were involved in a labor-management dispute regarding their "sanity" and patients who made diagnostic requests for legal purposes, the draft, and other reasons.

The second category included all other patients whom I saw for usually one and at most three interviews. This group includes five subcategories, the last two of which are important for future study:

a. Patients who were extremely paranoid but not overtly dangerous, without family or friends; they were referred to a therapist who was willing to work with them.

b. Patients for whom no therapy was recommended for various reasons.

c. Patients who were overtly psychotic and for whom hospitalization had to be recommended at once.

d. Patients for whom outpatient therapy was recommended but who refused it. Many excuses were given, including the lack of money (however, these patients also refused to be referred to a clinic), the demand for formal psychoanalysis, the wish for group therapy, and the desire for a religious therapist. Although appropriate referrals were given, these patients rarely followed them up.

e. Patients for whom psychotherapy was recommended and

accepted, but then they would never show up again; sometimes they would cancel by telephone, but often not. Most patients in this group were alcoholics or drug addicts. A few were teenagers: either they saw no need for therapy after thinking it over, or they were unable to return because their parents refused to permit or pay for therapy, even though they had cooperated with the diagnostic work-up.

The remaining patients in this subcategory presented a variety of nonpsychotic problems, usually borderline patients of character disorders. They simply gave no reason for their failure to return although initially they had appeared to be quite cooperative. It was impossible either to reach them by telephone or to get past their evasive answers, such as: "I remembered I had to go out of town, Doctor. I'll call when I get back." A typical beginning ploy of borderline patients was suddenly to schedule elective surgery and then be surprised and quite offended when their psychotherapy hours were not held open without charge for a month.

The third category included all patients who dropped out of therapy after at least three initial interviews but without mutual agreement to terminate. These patients were *not* all failures. The subcategories were:

a. Teenage patients who were taken out of treatment after one year (one or two sessions per week) by their parents; although they had made obvious substantial progress, their parents did not approve of their growing health and independence.

b. Patients with schizophrenic episodes and some with depressive episodes who gained symptomatic remission and good return of previous functioning capacity, but who refused to go further into uncovering psychotherapy. These were patients who had to leave me before I gave any signs of leaving them; they tended to have a very rigid and brittle ego structure.

c. Patients who revealed massive chronic fixed paranoid delusions, secretly held for many years and clearly inaccessible to treatment, at least by me; these patients usually terminated treatment after five to fifteen visits.

d. Patients (few in number) with a previous history of repeated hospitalization who became psychotic again during treatment and had to return to the hospital. These included some manic-depressives in a severe manic state, but most of them were schizophrenic.

e. Patients who dropped out after one to four months (five to sixteen sessions) because, in spite of repeated explanations, they expected fast results and therefore were easily disappointed. Most prominent in this group were oral characters, alcoholics, drug addicts, and patients with hypochondriacal complaints.

A few patients realized they could not really afford psychotherapy and admitted they had lied about their financial capacity because they secretly hoped to have an unusually quick treatment. The husbands of several women patients stopped paying for treatment, despite their initial agreement, because they had hoped for a quick change in their wives that did not materialize.

f. Patients who were outright failures. In spite of all my efforts, they either made no improvement or gradually went downhill over a period of fifty to two hundred sessions. In order to understand what happened, a patient-by-patient analysis is required; generally they were borderline patients, often with alcoholism or drug addiction. A few were homosexuals who had an increasing paranoid development that I could not check. Of those whom I could follow up, a small number reported definite improvement after leaving therapy; a few went on to see another therapist, with variable results, and two improved with subsequent group therapy.

The fourth category might be called the overtly successful cases; the subcategories of this group are most interesting:

a. Patients who were at first acutely schizophrenic but now in remission who terminated psychotherapy by mutual agreement after an average of one hundred and fifty sessions. Their adjustments seemed to be holding, and various circumstances made further uncovering treatment impractical.

b. Patients who received successful supportive psychotherapy. Although there was no basic personality change, integration and adaptation were greatly improved. Because of various factors it would have been impractical to attempt more than these important but limited goals.

c. Patients who showed obvious basic personality changes and successful functional and adaptational improvement after about four hundred to five hundred hours (four to four and one-half years).

d. Patients, initially alcoholic or psychotic, who now function quite well but have required supportive sessions from time to time over seven to ten years.

It is clear from this review that not all dropouts are failures in treatment and not all successes are terminable, according to my definitions. It is not easy to determine success or failure in psychotherapy nor to recognize the clinical danger periods for failure or dropping out.

Among teenagers, there are two characteristic danger periods. Early in the therapy (the first few sessions) there is often a *very high anxiety level,* which may lead the patient to drop out. Besides the usual anxiety at the beginning of treatment, a teenager often is not used to sitting down and talking with an adult, or to being listened to seriously. Teenagers are often pleasantly surprised to be granted the ordinary social amenities by the therapist. They are also exceptionally anxious because they feel an intense loyalty to their family and find it difficult (if not impossible) to reveal family secrets or speak disparagingly about even the worst of parents.

The second danger period for teenagers occurs when the patient begins to improve and show a sense of independence and identity (usually this happens after about a year of treatment, but could happen at any time). At this point some parents become quite upset and remove the patient from treatment. In my opinion, the problem of getting parent cooperation is the most difficult and frustrating task for the therapist who treats teenagers, and I know of no good techniques to solve this problem.

Patients who refuse treatment or unexpectedly fail to return after a diagnostic work-up represent an immediate and obvious failure at the outset. This failure is attributable to both the skill of the therapist and unconscious factors in the therapist and patient that reject either an alliance or psychotherapy. Therapists should try to follow up these patients as much as possible in order to learn more about them and the reason for the failure. Sometimes it is possible to determine what happened, as in the following two examples:

Dr. A. was a forty-year-old university professor who began to doubt his wife's fidelity a year and a half earlier. He began to follow her around and once found a wet spot on her panties which he called to her attention, insisting that it "smelled like sperm." At this point she demanded a separation. Dr. A. claimed that everyone "took her side." I gently but unwisely questioned him closely during the first interview about the smell of sperm and declared my neutrality about his wife's fidelity. Although he agreed that perhaps part of the problem was himself and made another appointment, he never returned. Obviously, my skepticism appeared as though I were taking his wife's side, and I learned from this experience not to pursue delusions with logic before a relationship has been established.

Mrs. B. was a twenty-nine-year-old mother of two, whose physician-husband was serving in Vietnam. During the previous six years of marriage she reported that she had been depressed and frigid and that she had yelled a great deal at her husband. She was clearly an oral character with a chronic depression. She reported that a couple of years earlier she had had one interview with a psychiatrist but did not like him and never returned; instead, she went to another psychiatrist who saw her once a week for a few months, and she felt that this had been helpful.

Describing herself as a "romantic," she said that she was lonely but felt that everything would be all right when her husband returned. She wanted some support and advice from a therapist to prepare herself for handling her husband when he returned. I tried to point out that she had a manipulating and controlling pattern, and I suggested a more ambitious goal for treatment, with interviews at least twice a week. Mrs. B. discussed this intelligently, seemed to understand, and agreed to come. The day of the next appointment, however, she called and asked me to refer her to another psychiatrist "for occasional supportive interviews"; she said she had decided to go to a graduate school and would have no time for regular psychotherapy. Obviously, I had misjudged Mrs. B.'s rigidity and overlooked her ambivalence apparent in her earlier experience with two psychiatrists, a pattern that she was now repeating. In this case, however, even if I had understood, it probably would not have made any difference; Mrs. B. *had* to repeat the pattern, and I was psychiatrist number one. Failure might have been precluded if I had been able to make an immediate interpretation.

Patients who must leave treatment before they have finished (even though they have improved) because they cannot stand the idea of termination by the therapist, patients who reveal a chronic paranoid structure, and patients (or their spouses) who insist in an almost delusional fashion on fast, magical results also present a danger period for dropping out; this usually appears after one to four months of treatment. If the therapist is aware of the danger and tries to prevent the dropout by repeated discussion with and interpretation to the patient in advance, there should certainly be improved results.

Outright failures, due to a basic defect in the therapist or the patient (or both), represent a tricky and stubborn problem as well as an unfortunate waste of time and money. The best hope for preventing these failures is to train psychotherapists adequately and encourage them to gain insight into themselves. From the point of view of the therapist, outright failures usually occur when there is no solid therapeutic alliance or when the therapist does not sufficiently recognize, interpret, and work through resistances before dealing with psychic content. In Chessick (1969a), I discuss the conduct of the therapist and the formation of the therapeutic alliance in detail. Greenson (1967) presents the technical aspects of dealing with resistance in an excellent fashion with many clinical illustrations. Briefly, he outlines the following general procedures:

1. Recognize the resistance.
2. Demonstrate the resistance to the patient.
   a. Allow it to become demonstrable by waiting for several instances.
   b. Intervene in such a way that will increase the resistance; help it to become demonstrable.
3. Clarify the motives and modes of resistance.
   a. What specific painful affect is making this patient resistant?

b. What particular instinctual impulse is causing the painful affect at this time?

c. What precise mode and method does the patient use to express his resistance?

4. Interpret the resistance.

a. What fantasies or memories are producing the affects and impulses behind the resistance?

b. Pursue the history and unconscious purposes of these affects, impulses, or events in and outside the analysis, including the past.

5. Interpret the mode of resistance.

a. Pursue this and similar modes of activity in and outside the analysis.

b. Trace the history and unconscious purposes of this activity in the patient's present and past.

6. Working through.

Repetitions and elaborations of steps 4. a. and b. and 5. a. and b.

Reviewing the outright failures in my practice indicates certain situations that can arise in psychotherapy which have been somewhat ignored in the literature. These situations carry the danger of a stalemate, and therefore could result in a tragic waste of hope, time, and money. Only awareness on the part of the therapist can help to prevent these situations from arising, but such awareness is only possible if the therapist has *more* than just the proper technical training.

To develop a reasonable working alliance, the therapist must first present himself in a reasonable and realistic fashion. This will automatically rule out a whole variety of bizarre procedures that are presently being foisted upon the public in the name of therapy. Furthermore, as Greenson (1967) has said:

Neither smugness, ritualism, timidity, authoritarianism, aloofness, nor indulgence have a place in the analytic situation. . . . The patient will be influenced not only by the content of our work but by how we work, the attitude, the manner, the mood, the atmosphere in which we work. He will react to and identify particularly with those aspects which are not necessarily conscious to us.

With this in mind, let me present some examples of outright failure from my practice that also illustrate situations of incipient stalemate. The first such situation occurs when the therapy is too vigorous, and ignores the patient's resistance to overwhelming and unacceptable dependent needs. A vigorous treatment that mobilizes such needs leads to increasing resistance, promotes acting-out, and eventually frightens the patient out of treatment. This is especially a problem with teenage patients, who often appear to be more intact than they actually are (but at other times they can appear to be less intact than they really are), thus fooling the therapist into believing that they are ready for uncovering therapy. A typical result is presented in the following case:

Miss C. was a sixteen-year-old Mexican girl who complained of depression and said that she had sniffed glue to the point of unconsciousness many times during the preceding two years. A female teacher at school decided to help her and began to spend much time with her after school talking about her problems; soon they were engaging in active homosexual play. The patient felt very guilty about this but clung to the teacher as the only source of warmth in her life; she had no interest in boys.

Her father worked nights and slept days; his only interest in his children seemed to be to hit them in the mouth when they said something he did not like. Her mother worked days and was exhausted all the time; she was a very shy and retiring person. A brother who was two years older was already boasting of a prison record and showed severe alcoholism; the patient was very fond of him and felt that her fate was intertwined with his. She had a number of incestuous dreams about her brother.

Miss C. was attractive, well mannered, appropriately dressed, and surprisingly able to discuss many issues intelligently. The contrast between her behavior in therapy and reports of what she was doing outside therapy was unbelievable. She appeared to be cooperative, involved, interested, and highly motivated to receive help. A psychiatrist had seen her for eight sessions about a year before she came to me and said she did not need further therapy. She began to bring up a considerable amount of material on the coldness of the atmosphere at home, her incestuous longings for her brother, her anger and guilt, and the psychodynamics of her depression and of the fascinating, multiply determined symptom of glue-sniffing. The patient eventually began to appear less depressed and to curtail her glue-sniffing. The homosexual relationship began to lose its ardor for both parties; it appeared that the patient was beginning to transfer her dependency to the therapy, with beneficial results.

After about fifty hours (two sessions per week), I went on a two-week vacation, giving the patient ample advance notice. Miss C. took this notice calmly and appropriately. After my return, however, the patient came on time to her first session and announced that she was stopping treatment because "I don't want to be dependent on anyone or anything." While I was gone apparently Miss C. realized that she missed me very much, and she could not accept those feelings. Nothing I said would change her mind and she stopped coming. A month later she called and asked for an appointment. I saw her, but all she did was sit quietly and report that she was sorry she had come. She refused to say any more and never came again. Later I heard she had tried group therapy but again dropped out.

The following is a similar case in which the mobilization of unacceptable dependent longings (this time in a sexual facade) seemed to play a major role in destroying treatment:

Mrs. D. was a shapely, twenty-six-year-old Jewish mother of a four-year-old boy. Her husband, two years older, worked for his father in a business that required him to put in about twelve hours a day, six days a week. He was the junior executive in this very lucrative business. The patient was pregnant when married and fought constantly with her husband when he was home. He insisted he was always right, saw nothing wrong with their married life, and resented her seeing a psychotherapist; at the same time he felt threatened by the therapist and frequently sent messages to him via his wife. Although Mrs. D. ostensibly entered therapy because of the arguments with her husband, it soon became clear that she was engaged in considerable sexual acting-out, which she also offered to do with the therapist; she was trying to use the therapist to manipulate her husband to meet her needs. At the same time she appeared to be intelligent, motivated, and personable; she seemed to cooperate fully with the treatment, although she could not form any sort of a genuine relationship with the therapist.

Mrs. D.'s mother had been repeatedly married. When the patient was six months old, her mother separated from her then-current husband and left the patient with grandparents in a small town so that she could work in the city. The grandparents were old-fashioned and severe and, as in the previous case, the atmosphere in the home was one of unrelieved coldness, including razor-strap beatings on the legs whenever she was naughty. Mrs. D.'s earliest memory was of being so short that she had to stand on tiptoes to see the food on the kitchen table, and her first dream was: "I slept past my appointment time and was very anxious; I thought to myself, Dr. Chessick will kill me if I'm late." This patient responded to my vacations with a great increase in her sexual acting-out.

The most remarkable fact about this therapy, which lasted about two hundred hours (one or two sessions a week), was that absolutely nothing happened at all! The patient continued unchanged in every way for two years, in spite of many kinds of interpretation. It was clear that she simply could not establish a relationship with me without revealing enormous sexual longings, which, of course, indicated a deep, passive dependency underneath. Although she kept coming and trying, no amount of discussion or interpretation could help; the patient, realizing the situation before I did, reduced her sessions to once a week. Even this was too much, and she finally stopped coming; she tried another therapist for a few weeks and then stopped seeing him also. A few months later the patient called me and sweetly suggested that we get together for "a drink or something" since I was no longer her therapist and thus not bound by any professional ethics. When I suggested that she needed further therapy, she was quite disappointed.

Clearly, it would have been better if I had not been fooled by this attractive, personable, and intelligent patient into thinking she could tolerate uncovering psychotherapy and the mobilization of her deep dependency in the transference. Several years of casual supportive psychotherapy, perhaps even marital counseling with her husband (if he would cooperate), would have been preferable. Of course, it is much easier to see this in retrospect, but both of these cases illustrate the danger of not carefully assessing *every* aspect of the patient's ego capacities and remaining on the alert for signs that the patient is really not tolerating the therapeutic work — no matter how hopeful he may appear to be.

Of course, the classical example of this kind of case, the first (and in many ways still the best and most instructive) failure in psychotherapy was reported by Freud (1913). He wrote about Dora immediately after she abruptly left therapy, ostensibly to illustrate the importance of dream interpretation in psychoanalysis and to outline the psychodynamics of hysteria. Dora left treatment after three months, stating she had decided in advance to give herself "until the New Year" to be cured. However, as Freud recognized, the transference aspects of the case undoubtedly led her to drop out. The case should be read in its entirety, but is presented in summary form by Stafford-Clark (1966), who reports the difficulty Freud had in deciding to publish the manuscript, postponing it for four years. It is also noteworthy that, as in the two cases described above, Dora returned later (after fifteen months) for a single additional contact with the therapist but, "One glance at her face, however, was enough to tell me that she was not in earnest over her request."

It is easy to debate whether Dora should have been diagnosed as a hysteric or a borderline patient (Chessick, 1969a, 1971a). Certainly the reaction of Deutsch (1957), an outstanding psychoanalyst who saw her many years later, was typical of that often experienced with borderline patients. He writes:

In the first interview where the patient was seen about twenty years after she had broken off treatment with Freud, she continued to complain of ear noises, dizziness and attacks of migraine. She then started a tirade about her husband's indifference, about her sufferings, and how unfortunate her marital life has been. She felt her only son had begun to neglect her. He often stayed out late at night and she suspected he had become interested in girls. She always waited listening until he came home. She expressed a great amount of hostile feelings towards her husband, especially her disgust with marital sex life. Dora's fate took the course that Freud had predicted twenty-four years after the three months analysis with her. She clung to her son with the same reproachful demands she made on her husband, who had died tortured by her vengeful behavior.

Deutsch described her as "one of the most repulsive hysterics" he had ever met. At any rate, one could certainly argue that Dora's famous second dream was a long resistance dream, based on the wish to dominate the hour and hiding the secret that she was planning to drop out of treatment. Freud's analysis of the dream is not convincing; he recognized that therapy had mobilized Dora's powerful sexual drives towards the therapist, with a corresponding rage at men (whom she considered evil and undependable) and a typical wish for revenge.

As a patient's defenses are undermined in uncovering therapy, the pressure of unconscious drives focus on the therapist in the transference. To deal with this there must be a suitable therapeutic alliance, correct understanding and interpretation of the transference, and insight into the countertransference. In 1900, when Freud treated Dora, all these aspects were barely recognized; in fact, the case is amazing in that, as Jones (1955) points out, anyone would "take the data of psychology so seriously." Dora's case typified what we still encounter today. As Freud himself noted:

> If cruel impulses and revengeful motives, which have already been used in the patient's ordinary life for maintaining her symptoms, become transferred on to the physician during treatment, before he has had time to detach them from himself

by tracing them back to their sources, then it is not to be wondered at if the patient's condition is unaffected by his therapeutic efforts. For how could the patient take a more effective revenge than by demonstrating upon her own person the helplessness and incapacity of the physician?

The second type of situation that poses a danger of failure (or at least stalemate) was also anticipated by Freud, in what must be one of the most frank, moving, and poignant passages in all of his writing — also from the case of Dora. Certain patients, especially borderline ones, confront us with very difficult decisions about gratifications in the transference. I have referred to this elsewhere (Chessick, 1968b) as a "crucial dilemma" for the therapist. When we ask these patients to become involved in therapy with us, we automatically mobilize their deep anxieties about penetration and annihilation, and strange reactions occur. In addition, these patients have often become locked in a "neurosis of abandonment" (Odier, 1956) before coming to therapy; thus, the process of therapy threatens their neurotic binds, which had been formed to protect them against unbearable anxiety. The threat to these protective binds is immediate, sometimes arising from just the idea of having therapy, and there is no time to work through the situation. Continuation of the therapy becomes touch and go from session to session, and the therapist has to decide to what extent he should offer himself as a "real object" (Tarachow, 1963).

Here is the situation as Freud experienced it in 1900:

No one who, like me, conjures up the most evil of those half-tamed demons that inhabit the human breast, and seeks to wrestle with them, can expect to come through the struggle unscathed. Might I perhaps have kept the girl under my treatment if I myself had acted a part, if I had exaggerated the importance to me of her staying on, and had shown a warm personal interest in her — a course which, even after allowing for my position as her physician, would have been tantamount to providing her with a substitute for the affection she longed for? I do not know. Since in every case a portion of the factors that are encountered under the form of resistance remains unknown, I have always avoided acting a part, and have contented myself with practising the humbler arts of psychology. In spite of every theoretical interest and of every endeavour to be of assistance as a physician, I keep the fact in mind that there must be some limits set to the extent to which psychological influence may be used, and I respect as one of these limits the patient's own will and understanding.

I will present some clinical examples from my own practice of failure in this type of situation. Miss E. was a very attractive twenty-three-year-old Jewish girl who was referred to me by a charity organization. Therapy one and one-half years earlier had ended in stalemate after several months, with the patient owing a substantial amount of money to the therapist which she never paid. She complained of weird sensations in her head, including a popping and snapping in her ears, and a feeling that she was either numb in her head or that the blood was rushing in. She was taking an assortment of pills — I couldn't get all of the details — from various physicians for reducing, although her figure couldn't have been more shapely. She reported a number of affairs with older men who "took care of her" during the past few years, but she had an obvious mounting anxiety about her future.

My first impression was that she was another Dora, but the situation became increasingly ominous for, as Miss E. came in once or twice a week, she began to report a whole variety of phobic, compulsive, psychosomatic, confusing, and even paranoid symptoms. At the same time our relationship seemed to be important to her, for under the influence of treatment she gave up her affairs and took a job as a stenographer for the first time. It seemed as if there were a serious paranoid core underneath the variety of symptoms and that long supportive psychotherapy would be needed, but that the patient would eventually respond.

Miss E. had an older and more successful sister. Her father, a taxi driver, had a teasing kind of sexual relationship with the patient. They slept together until she was twelve years old; now she would parade around the house in her underwear, which would provoke screaming rage from him. The mother seemed to be a cold, timid, and frigid woman. The patient lived with her parents in a tiny apartment and was desperately lonely.

The patient worked with me for about two years. By the end of the first year she began to be asked for dates by men who were definite marriage prospects. It gradually dawned on the patient that she was improving (at least in her functioning), and that she had a chance to marry and move away from her parents. At that point she started to come later and later for the therapy sessions, sometimes arriving just for the last five minutes. She began to develop some definite ideas of reference with respect to a few of the women in her office. Therapy degenerated into an effort to allay her anxiety so that she could continue to come, but nothing I said did any good; even chlorpromazine produced nothing but side effects. I experienced the pain of watching a previously hopeful psychotherapy patient deteriorate in front of my eyes while I sat by helplessly. After several months of coming very late to each session, the patient finally stopped coming altogether; she appeared to be about the same state as when she started therapy. She left owing me money, as with her previous psychotherapist.

In this case, when the threat of mature sexual functioning and the prospect of leaving her parents appeared, and when her sexual feelings were mobilized in the transference, the patient became overwhelmed with anxiety. Probably the same thing had happened in her earlier treatment. In trying to deal with anxiety, the therapist is in a vicious circle if the patient has no insight and is preschizophrenic. The therapist's passivity leads to an increase in the patient's anxiety and a consequent dropping out of treatment. The therapist's activity increases the patient's anxiety because it stirs up a sexualized response to the therapist's interest; in the transference his actions are experienced as suspiciously seductive. The result is a retreat to homosexual outlets with a paranoid defense. The patient must then choose whether to become severely paranoid or to stop therapy! In the case of Miss E., the patient will go from affair to affair and from therapist to therapist; the circle is unbreakable since there is no chance for the ego to develop an awareness in the face of her extreme anxieties. Miss E.'s situation was further complicated by the tight neurotic bind with her parents and her inability to move away from them.

This leads to the problem in which the therapist finds himself in the unenviable position of coming between the abandonee and his object in a "neurosis of abandonment" (Odier, 1956). Many borderline patients form a relationship in which they must be absolutely sure at all times they are loved by the object of their neurosis. Thus, life becomes a series of ups and downs for the patient, depending upon the signals received from the object. As Odier explains:

> The object shows distraction, lack of attention or reticence; criticism or a justified reproach; an absent-minded, sad, or severe look; a slightly brusque gesture; a rough and perhaps explosive tone of voice; mockery; "a passing cloud"; and especially silence which is almost always interpreted as ominous; pleasant things which happen at the wrong moment; teasing, a trick or a joke . . . not to be there at the right time.

This "neurosis of abandonment" relationship protects the patient from severe annihilation anxiety through mechanisms of magical thinking, well described by Odier. Yet the severe ups and downs that obviously haunt the patient often bring him into treatment. If an attempt is made to break up the "neurosis of abandonment," overwhelming anxiety develops and the treament ends, as in the previous case. If no attempt is made, and interpretations and discussion are not forthcoming, nothing happens and the treatment is stalemated. Sometimes the patient can transfer his dependency to the therapist; this is most hopeful because then it can be worked through. Usually, however, he is not able to do this because he must be around the object physically a great deal, preferably all the time.

The therapist who is not aware runs three risks here. First, if he does not recognize that the patient has developed such a relationship with a chosen object, he misses the essence of the case entirely. Second, it is disastrous not to recognize that the patient's anxiety level is becoming unbearable as therapy threatens to separate him from the object. Thus, from the point of view of the reasonable therapist, it might appear that a little common sense would lead the patient to give up an obviously painful and destructive relationship with the object, and so he might try to discuss the harmful effects of the relationship with the patient. Third, and perhaps worst of all, is for the therapist not to recognize that the "neurosis of abandonment" is being transferred to himself. Thus, he misses the opportunity to really work through the problem, thereby enabling it to explode. I know of one case in which the therapist discovered to his horror that the patient had purchased a house next door to his own! The following two cases illustrate these problems.

Mr. F. was an intelligent, "nice Jewish boy" of twenty-one; at nineteen he had become intimate with and wanted to marry an older divorcée who finally jilted him for an older and more successful man. Mr. F. became filled with rage and depression and had to be hospitalized for three weeks. When he felt better he took a vacation trip to Europe for several months at his parents' expense. Shortly after his return, he met another girl, slipping rather quickly again into the classical "neurosis of abandonment" picture. The girl, who was an actress, caused him many ups and downs; eventually he made several feeble suicide attempts and had to be hospitalized for short periods. The patient could only function in a minimal way as a street social worker at a very low salary; school was impossible.

The parents, of traditional Jewish middle class background, were absolutely desperate and filled with guilt as they watched the steady deterioration of all the hopes they had invested in their only son. Two older children, both girls, were doing well, but the son was the golden boy of the family; indeed, he was quite intelligent, articulate, and personable. The mother controlled the family by manipulation and "serious intellectual discussions." The father was rather depreciated as a businessman who had to put in long hours at the store.

Mr. F. had considerable identity confusion and the feeling that he was not masculine enough to do all the things he wanted to do (in order to live up to his parents' expectations). He wanted to be active in many social causes, have boundless energy, be a good athlete, and make lots of money. He had a secret longing for affection from his father, who seemed to be the only source of affection in the family; at the same time he felt that men are weak and at the mercy of women, which was what he acted out in his "neurosis of abandonment." His first dream was of having sexual intercourse with a girl cousin, while a leering old man was watching and annoying him. His earliest memory was of walking with his father on his afternoon off.

Psychotherapy with this patient was like riding a roller coaster. For one hundred and fifty hours during a two-year period, Mr. F. went up and down with the whims of his girl friend, occasionally requiring brief hospitalization when he was flooded with rage. The therapy remained an absolute stalemate, although sometimes I thought there was a glimmer of hope when the patient seemed to identify with me or with certain other male figures that he could look up to. But absolutely nothing could be done about the girl; the tight bind remained even though the patient did not want it and understood its effect on him. No matter what approach I tried, my interpretations remained on the level of intellectual discussion.

Finally, in spite of his parents' protest (for they appreciated the fact that I was the first therapist their son remained with for any extended period of time), we terminated the treatment by mutual agreement. The patient was getting nowhere and we both knew it. Before that I had tried to get the patient to come more often, but had failed; I was unable to follow up the experiences of this patient. Patients like Mr. F. provide considerable frustration and disappointment to the psychotherapist; there is a feeling of waste and tragedy for them as well.

Miss G. was referred to me by a psychoanalyst who was seeing her boy friend — the object of her "neurosis of abandonment" — in formal psychoanalysis. There were two drawbacks in the situation. One was that her boy friend was in serious trouble with the Internal Revenue Service and was therefore missing about two-thirds of his psychoanalytic sessions although he was paying for them. The other was that I was flattered by the referral and so I tried to do a good job to demonstrate my skill.

Miss G.'s presenting complaint showed itself in her first dream: "The earth was caving away and I was trying to stay on the sidewalk." It was clear that this abandonee's object would soon be in the penitentiary for a long time and that this thought was intolerable; her sense of insecurity was greatly heightened and even now, at the first sign of rejection by her boy friend, she went into literal screaming fits outside his door.

Miss G. was a twenty-three-year-old, slim, attractive blonde. Her parents had to marry after she was conceived; she had one sister (two years younger) who was apparently doing well. This patient's childhood seemed to be an utter chaos. Her father was a high-pressure businessman who was simply never home; his store was open every day and every night. He was constantly dissatisfied and always talking about moving to California. Her mother apparently spent a lot of time at the store also, and the parents made a lot of money. The children were largely left to fend for themselves; I was reminded of the children in a Negro ghetto, although Miss G. and her sister lived in a fine neighborhood.

She dropped out of high school and secured a variety of jobs, including window model at a local health club and salesgirl. She had passing relationships with a number of men before she met her current boy friend. She claimed that he was the only man who ever meant anything to her and that she was determined to marry him and spend all her time with him. He didn't seem to feel the same toward her; at that time, he seemed to be rather harassed by her and interested in other women.

Miss G.'s psychotherapy, for the approximate fifty hours that it lasted, was like watching a low-grade cops-and-robbers movie. The patient spent all of her time tracking her boy friend around to see if he was cheating; if she even had a hint that he was seeing someone else, her panic was extreme and dramatic. When he wasn't cheating, she was deliriously happy and spent her time camping in his apartment. The patient never showed the slightest response to anything I said; my only function for her was as somebody to talk to when she was unhappy with her boyfriend.

When I exerted pressure on her to discuss the destructive aspects of this relationship and to get her to recognize what her boyfriend was really like, Miss G. simply stopped coming. Later on I received a card from her. She had moved to the town near the prison where her boyfriend had been incarcerated. At no time in the therapy did the patient even admit that anything was wrong with her.

The third (and final) situation that may lead to outright failure (and that deserves more attention in the literature) arises from the treatment by a male psychotherapist of a male borderline patient who is also overtly homosexual. There are two potential dangers here. Either there will be a mobilization of the homosexual yearnings in the transference, which can lead to unbearable anxiety and a subsequent breaking off of treatment (exactly analogous to the first situation described above with women), or there will be a sublimated and intellectualized latching onto the therapist. In the latter case the psychotherapist must deal with his own anxieties about homosexual feelings in both himself and the patient, and he must avoid an interminable, stalemated psychotherapy. I have seen *many* examples of lengthy, expensive, and useless psychoanalyses and psychotherapies of sublimated homosexuals.

Here is an example of each danger from my own practice. Mr. H. was a twenty-seven-year-old overt homosexual who began his homosexual activities four years earlier, after his father died of a heart attack. At that time he actively courted and seduced a social worker who was supposed to be giving him supportive psychotherapy, and they developed a homosexual relationship in which the patient repeatedly performed fellatio on the social worker but refused in his turn "to be messed with." Apparently the social worker came to feel quite guilty because, although he continued the homosexual relationship, he told the patient that he ought to seek another therapist and gave him some names. Since one of these therapists was busy, he referred the patient to me (I was not on the original list). Thus, the patient came to see me while he was still actively engaged in the homosexual relationship with the first therapist. He knew that things were not right and seemed serious about making certain changes in his life. He was not in a "neurosis of abandonment" with the social worker; as a matter of fact it turned out to be the other way around. His presenting complaint was depression; the patient had majored in psychology in college and had a substantial intellectual understanding of his plight.

Mr. H.'s history was fairly typical. His father was a cruel over-bearing man who frequently beat the patient and locked him in the coal bin. His mother was essentially disinterested, and he had many siblings. In this state of affect-starvation the patient eventually got the idea that sucking the penis of an older male would be wonderful; it would gratify everybody and make the older man nicer to him. He had never been interested in girls. After graduating from college, he began teaching in the public schools.

Shortly before my summer vacation we began discussing some-thing about the dynamics of his situation, especially his fear of aggression (castration) from the male. Mr. H. appeared to be in-terested and cooperative; he came to his sessions regularly and even began to consider giving up his homosexual partner. When I returned from vacation he came to the first session with his right arm and hand all bandaged up. He had spent the vacation in the country and had caught his hand in a fertilizing machine, badly mangling the hand and arm. I took this as a serious warning, and the patient began to bring up historical material that made him look increasingly schizoid. Apparently he spent his childhood alone, riding back and forth on the elevated trains. He had many suicidal fantasies. I switched to an increasingly supportive role and the patient stabilized and left treatment in about the same condition that he had come.

It was clear that the patient's situation had become explosive and that further attempts at uncovering psychotherapy would have led either to suicide or to an overt schizophrenic breakdown. The material he brought up pointed to great anxiety over shifting his deep affectional longings away from his homosexual acting-out and into therapy in the transference; he had simply no capacity to deal with this anxiety except to destroy himself or to crack up.

Mr. I. was a twenty-two-year-old man with a Jewish father and a Lutheran mother, but with no siblings. He was the most educated and intelligent patient I have ever met, a top student at the University of Chicago. He had been an active homosexual for five years before coming to see me, and he was one of my earliest patients in private practice. He came twice a week, and later switched to once a week for financial reasons, totaling about two hundred hours. He finally stopped therapy, owing me money, and insisted he wanted a famous psychoanalyst and a classical psychoanalysis.

Mr. I.'s father worked in a factory and had been stooped over for many years because of a spine injury. He was a "very sweet little man." His mother was described as stern, rigid, and hard to please and to live with. Until he went to the University of Chicago he lived with his parents in another city; the overt purpose of going to Chicago was to get away from them and begin active homosexuality, a decision he made deliberately.

Psychotherapy with this patient was like reading Fenichel's *The Psychoanalytic Theory of Neuroses* (1945). The patient presented a wide array of neurotic, psychosomatic, drug-taking, and many other acting-out symptoms, for which he was able to supply remarkably intelligent and deep-sounding interpretations; none of these led to improvement of any kind. I let the patient do most of the talking and did not show too much agreement or disagreement with his interpretations. I hoped to form a supportive relationship with him in order to help him stabilize and direct his life; I would have been quite satisfied with this result since this borderline patient did not show any interest in changing his homosexual orientation. I thought this might be possible because I genuinely liked him and he seemed to be cooperative and interested in treatment.

Mr. I. was taking combinations of all kinds of drugs in relatively small but unknown amounts; he largely stole them from the university hospital. He tried out almost everything in the pharmacopoeia and presented me with long dissertations on the effect of each. He regarded himself as an experimental object; he was very sick and very interesting.

After about a year with no apparent change, I began to spend considerable time thinking about this patient's sessions to see if I was missing anything. Suddenly it occurred to me that I had overlooked the obvious in myself — almost every session with this patient was marked by an extraordinary sensation of sleepiness that I had to fight off consciously. I had only experienced this once before with a patient; when I was a resident, I had an overtly homosexual schizophrenic patient who was making obvious seductive overtures to me.

It was now clear that Mr. I. had slipped into an intellectualized and sublimated unconscious homosexual relationship with me, which was in turn arousing countertransference anxiety; sleepiness was my particular defense in this situation. When I became aware of what he was really doing in therapy, and attempted to confront him with this, his cooperativeness changed and therapy became very stormy. He increased his drug consumption and acted more and more bizarre. I was no longer sleepy.

As the patient became aware that I would no longer permit the unconscious interaction to continue without focusing upon it in therapy, he began to insist on seeing another therapist; finally, as I have already reported, he left treatment to find a famous psychoanalyst. As a matter of fact he did contact a highly renowned psychoanalyst who held an important and prestigious position in the area and had a few sessions with him. Of course, nothing came of it, for the analyst had my report and soon recognized what was going on. So ended one of the most egregious and tragic failures I have ever encountered. At latest report, the patient is still continuing exactly as before. At one time I testified as to his mental condition in order to keep him from going to jail for possession of marihuana, but this was the last contact I had with him.

The reader must not assume that if only the therapist is humane, insightful, intelligent, aware of countertransference problems, and empathic with his patient, all will be well. Obviously, there are many factors in a patient that may preclude successful psychotherapy, sometimes only with certain therapists, sometimes with any therapist. Furthermore, an optimal psychic field can only *reduce* the incidence of failure; in some situations it may *itself* produce a reaction in the patient that can lead to failure. Greenson

(1967) provided a remarkable example of this, in which Mr. Z. first illustrates the kind of failure in therapeutic alliance that can occur with a psychotherapist who has the proper technical training but is not humane; later Mr. Z. illustrates how Greenson's far more optimal psychic field itself became a homosexual threat in the transference, with the very same danger as described above in the first example of outright failure, where the mobilization of unacceptable longings threatened to destroy the treatment.

A young man, Mr. Z., came to me for analysis after having spent two and a half years with an analyst in another city in an analysis which had left him almost completely untouched. He had obtained certain insights, but he had the distinct impression that his former analyst really disapproved of infantile sexuality, even though the young man realized that analysts were not supposed to be contemptuous of it. In the preliminary interviews the young man told me that he had the greatest difficulty in talking about masturbation and often consciously withheld this information from his previous analyst. He had informed the latter about the existence of many conscious secrets, but nevertheless stubbornly refused to divulge them. He never wholeheartedly gave himself up to free association, and there were many hours of long silence in which he and his analyst both remained mute. The patient's manner of relating to me, however, his history, and my general clinical impression led me to believe that he was analyzable, despite the fact that he had not been able to form a working alliance with his first analyst.

I undertook to analyze Mr. Z. and learned a great deal about his negative reactions to his previous analyst, some of which stemmed from his way of conducting the analysis. For example, in one of the first hours on the couch the patient took out a cigarette and lit it. I asked him what he was feeling when he decided to light the cigarette. He answered petulantly that he knew he was not supposed to smoke in his previous analysis and how he supposed that I too would forbid this. I told Mr. Z. that I wanted to know what feelings, ideas, and sensations were going on in him at the moment that he decided to light the cigarette. He then revealed that he had become somewhat frightened in the hour and to shield this anxiety from my view he decided to light the cigarette.

I replied that it was preferable for such feelings and ideas to be expressed in words instead of actions because then I would understand more precisely what was going on in him. He realized then that I was not forbidding him to smoke but only pointing out that it was more helpful to the process of being analyzed if he expressed himself in words and feelings. He contrasted this with his first analyst who told him before he went to the couch that it was customary not to smoke on the couch. There was no explanation for this and the patient felt that his first analyst was being arbitrary.

In a later hour Mr. Z. asked me whether I was married. I countered by asking him what did he imagine about that. He hesitantly revealed that he was torn between two sets of fantasies, one that I was a bachelor who loved his work and lived only for his patients; the other fantasy was that I was a happily married man with many children. He then went on spontaneously to tell me that he hoped I was happily married because then I would be in a better position to help him with his sexual problems. Then Mr. Z. corrected himself and said it was painful to think of me as having sexual relations with my wife because that was embarrassing and none of his business. I then pointed out to him how, by not answering his question and by asking him instead to tell his fantasies about the answer, he revealed to us what his curiosity was about. I told him I would not answer questions when I felt that more was to be gained by my keeping silent and letting him associate to his own question.

At this point Mr. Z. became somewhat tearful and after a short pause he told me that in the beginning of his previous analysis he had asked many questions. His former analyst never answered, nor did he ever explain why he was silent. He felt his analyst's silence as a degradation and humiliation and now realized that his own later silences were a retaliation for this imagined injustice. Somewhat later he realized that he had identified with his first analyst's supposed contempt. Mr. Z. felt disdain for his analyst's prudishness and at the same time was full of severe self-reproach for his own sexual practices which he then projected back onto the analyst.

It was very instructive to me to see how an identification with the previous analyst based on fear and hostility led to a distortion of the working relationship instead of an effective working alliance. The whole atmosphere of the first analysis was contaminated by hostile, mistrustful, retaliative feelings and attitudes. This turned out to be a repetition of the patient's behavior toward his father, a point the first analyst had recognized and interpreted. The analysis of this transference resistance, however, was ineffectual due in part to the fact that the former analyst worked in such a way as to constantly justify the patient's infantile neurotic behavior and so furthered the invasion of the working alliance by the transference neurosis.

I worked with Mr. Z. for approximately four years and almost from the very beginning a relatively effective working alliance was established. However, my manner of conducting analysis, which seemed to him to indicate some genuine human concern for his welfare and respect for his position as a patient also mobilized important transference resistances in a later phase of the analysis. In the third year of his analysis with me I began to realize that despite what seemed to be a good working alliance and a strong transference neurosis, there were many areas of the patient's outside life which did not seem to change commensurate with the analytic work. Eventually I was able to discover that the patient had developed a subtle but specific inhibition in doing analytic work outside of the analytic hour. When Mr. Z. became upset outside the hour, he would ask himself what upset him. Usually he would succeed in recalling the situation in question. Sometimes he even might recall the meaning of that event which I had given him at some previous point, but this insight would be relatively meaningless to him; it felt foreign, artificial, and remembered by rote. It was not his insight; it was mine, and therefore had no living significance for him. He was therefore relatively blank about the meaning of the events which upset him.

Apparently, although he seemed to have established a working alliance with me in the analytic situation, this did not remain outside of the hour. Analysis revealed that the patient did not allow himself to assume any attitude, approach, or point of view that was like mine outside of the analytic hour. He felt that to permit himself to do so would be tantamount to admitting that I had entered into him. This was intolerable because Mr. Z. felt this to be a homosexual assault, a repetition of several childhood and adolescent traumata. Slowly we were able to uncover how the patient had sexualized and aggressified the process of introjection.

This new insight was the starting point for the patient to

begin to learn to discriminate among the different varieties of
"taking in." Gradually the patient was able to re-establish a
homosexual-free identification with me in terms of adopting
an analytic point of view. Thus, a working relationship which
had been invaded by the transference neurosis was once again
relatively free of infantile neurotic features. The previous insights which had remained ineffectual eventually led to a
significant and lasting change.

Greenson's case illustrates the extreme difficulty of doing
effective uncovering psychotherapy even when the patient is
apparently cooperating and the psychotherapist is well trained and
humane. Imagine the situation, therefore, when the therapist is
poorly trained or actually indifferent to what he is doing. One of
the most unfortunate rationalizations put forward today for poor
training is that therapeutic results are non-specific, that is, they are
merely the result of two people who happen to click with each
other or the consequence of a therapist who happens to be pleasant
and friendly. No attitude could be more destructive to the development or a rational and scientific approach to psychotherapy, for
if this were true, then no training would be necessary at all — it
would only be necessary to select friendly people to be therapists.
Some authors actually advocate this, but I believe it really hides
their frustration over the extreme difficulty of deciding what
factors are significant in any given psychotherapy encounter.

Just because we are ignorant of how psychotherapy heals or
fails does *not* mean that it is impossible to understand specifically
what factors contribute to healing or failure in psychotherapy or
to try to study and control these factors scientifically. The present
trend away from individual psychotherapy is partly due to the
kinds of frustrations and failures met, for example, in the various
cases presented earlier. Failures and frustrations, especially in working with patients over long periods of time, take a definite psychic
toll on the therapist. As a result, some therapists stop doing
individual psychotherapy altogether, some limit their practice, and
some just try to avoid the intense concentration required by assum-
ing a nonchalant attitude. A serious problem arises when such

therapists communicate their disillusionment to neophytes, especially since many applicants for training as psychiatrists or psychotherapists are only too eager to avoid the basic difficulties that must be faced in trying to understand and heal people with emotional problems.

This problem was recognized some years ago by Aubrey Lewis (Hoch, 1948), who wrote: "It is my opinion that a considerable amount of poor psychotherapy will be practiced from about now through the next ten years at least." Lewis pointed out how the need for more psychotherapists had stimulated many a middle-aged physician to give up his general practice or specialty.

> . . . where he is dissatisfied or in which he may not have been too successful, and seek training in psychiatry. . . . Obviously, such as these. and they are numerous, have no insight into the complications or significance of the psychiatric field. . . . In the face of this situation we must formulate and adhere to rather rigid educational standards and not hesitate to publicize this attitude. To comprehend the nature of the mind requires a wide knowledge of a number of scientific and social fields in addition to that of medicine.

Unfortunately, there has been no significant change in this situation since 1948, and so we often see the nightmare described by Lewis where beginners or untrained therapists "eager to achieve results as quickly as possible, often push themselves into the problem and become entangled in a maze of theoretic mechanisms in which they become increasingly impatient, frustrated and disappointed in results to the detriment of the patient and to their own success." Just because untrained therapists become frustrated in their efforts or because middle-aged therapists become tired of their work is no reason to assume that psychotherapy cannot be effective, specific, and teachable. We must learn from our failures what our own personal shortcomings are and what we must warn our students about; failure in psychotherapy, if properly analyzed, can become a stepping-stone to further knowledge rather than a reason for discouragement and retreat into a nonchalant attitude.

The problem is immensely complicated by the fact that many people are doing psychotherapy today without either any scientific training or any conception of a "physicianly vocation" (Stone, 1961). As Lewis pointed out: "The treatment of the mentally ill can be improved only by the slow, persistent, long continued labors of the scientific physician. It is a kind of labor the nature of which those undisciplined in science can form no conception." I hope that the cases of outright failure in psychotherapy presented here will contribute to an understanding of the complexities of psychotherapy and the kind of training the psychotherapist must have.

6

Vicissitudes in the Life of the Psychotherapist

It has been stated that the psychiatrist is expected to be stable and secure enough to be consistently aware of and in control of what he conveys to his patients in words and mindful of what he may convey by empathy. Also his need for operations aimed at his own security and satisfaction should not interfere with his ability to listen consistently to patients, with full alertness to their communications per se and, if possible, to the unworded implications of their verbalized communications.

Frieda Fromm-Reichmann,
Principles of Intensive Psychotherapy

This chapter presents an example of failure in psychotherapy that took place by the second interview. The therapist is a second-year resident in psychiatry who knew nothing about the patient prior to the first interview, and the patient is a tall, thin, prim, and proper Negro woman. The interviews were held in a psychiatric hospital and were tape-recorded and observed by a seminar group of residents and one or two senior consultants. They illustrate many beginner's mistakes as well as the dramatic effect the therapist can have on the patient's ultimate acceptance or rejection of psycho-therapy. The patient is very difficult and the interviews are frustrating, but I felt it would be better to illustrate beginner's mistakes with interviews showing both good and bad technique rather than with interviews demonstrating obvious and easily rectifiable errors.

These interviews can also be discussed in terms of the psychic field presented by the therapist to the patient. There are repeated collisions between the yearning, confused, and needy field of the patient and the anxious field of the resident, who is overly pre-occupied with technique; these collisions clearly demonstrate the impact of these two fields — with a negative or repelling result. It was unfortunate that the resident did not recognize the feelings of this confused, borderline-psychotic, Negro woman in all their humane, sociological, and technical ramifications. Instead, he was largely a doctor taking her history. For those who may feel that my comments are too critical of the resident, the resident was myself fifteen years ago.

FIRST INTERVIEW

THERAPIST: Good morning.
PATIENT: *(Smiling radiantly):* Good morning!
THERAPIST: You look happy.
PATIENT: Oh, I am happy to see the sunshine. Ah, the view to the east here in the morning is lovely.
THERAPIST: Oh.
PATIENT: Down at our end it seems a little bit cloudy.
THERAPIST: I wonder if you could speak a little bit louder, please . . .

(This comment is related to the therapist's anxiety about the sessions being tape-recorded and observed. This anxiety subsides as the interview proceeds.)

PATIENT: Oh, sure. The view, I was saying, on the east, as we came out toward the elevator, is very pretty. Down at our end of the building it seems a little cloudy yet, and that's why I was smiling.

THERAPIST: I see.

PATIENT: Also, I am glad I am seeing a doctor at last because I've been so anxious to have some O.T. privileges. The gang seems to have so much fun and I'm left reading my eyes out for about three hours a day, and I do want to go down and do something with my hands. This idleness is wearing me down.

THERAPIST: Well, can you tell me how you happened to come to the hospital. What seems to be the trouble?

(The therapist's response could set the stage for failure. The patient requested something concrete [O.T. privileges]. The therapist does not acknowledge this request at all but goes on, in a stereotyped way, to the standard history-gathering questions. As in chess, an inferior opening move will be paid for later in the game! The message to the patient could be interpreted by her as "You feed me first.")

PATIENT: My own personal opinion?

THERAPIST: Yes.

PATIENT: Ah, I think that the difficulty with me is attached to the climacteric, the menopause, and, ah, the tensions under which I have been living during the past year have more or less brought me to a state where I, uh, couldn't remember things. Ah, you know, the usual symptoms — I wept very easily, I became overanxious when left alone, I became suspicious of people's motives when mostly they were kind. Ah, I think I took life a little bit too seriously. Coupled with that, the ah, the death of my mother some years ago, ah, being repressed since 1949, has . . . I've only now become able to grieve nor-

124

mally for her. And, ah, I think that, with the glandular changes, brought about a crisis, and here I am. That's the brief story. There are many things, I suppose, that in my background would point to, ah, facing up to death in the family. And then, there's ah,, ah, physical fatigue that's been piling up for years. I was married in '40 when I was still in school, and my husband was called to active duty in '41. My first child was born in '41, my second in '42, and we traveled from the East coast to the West in that year. The next two and a half years were travel also while he was overseas. Then there's been uh, aside from the usual work in one place, there was teaching in, in Virginia, social work in Canton, Ohio and . . . during which period my father died, there was college teaching at Central State College in Ohio, and the return of my husband and his four years in school while I taught. Then, the first job in May-wood here . . . the first home we actually had in '51 was ten years after we were married. So that those ten years were not just physically tiring,, but emotionally — sort of debilitating too. So, here I am here.

(Diagnostically it is significant that the patient goes along with the therapist's wishes and begins to give a lot of intellectualized historical material without protesting about the O.T. privileges.)

THERAPIST: That's right. That ended in '51, correct?
PATIENT: The ten years . . .
THERAPIST: Ten years.
PATIENT: . . . ended in '51, and then began . . .
THERAPIST: This is '56.
PATIENT: Well, the '51 years were, uh, a series of little things. Uh, I was unemployed for the first time in my life for the year '51 to '52, and the children then, the two that we had, a boy and a girl, were in grammar school, and I conceived the brilliant idea that I should be working, so I did get a very pleasant job, and a challenging one, as a biochemist at the veterans hospital there, in December, '52. I worked there three years. Enjoyed every minute of it and, uh, the children grew, pros-

pered in school, my husband's job seemed to be a good one, although he did have some personality clashes there, mainly, uh, the adjustment of the non-white to the white research group was pretty tough, at first.

THERAPIST: Now, that was your husband's problem.

(This was a typical example of a gratuitous comment by the therapist. One can only guess what he had in mind — it seems to be a beginning impatience with the historical material.)

PATIENT: Yeah. Yeah. And at home, uh, I had very little conflict — uh, I felt better than I had in years. Until, uh, the summer of '55. Now, during that summer, I became pregnant for the fir —, for the third time, after almost fourteen years. During that summer also, we made a long trip back to what we call home. Canton, Ohio, is my family home. And, it was there that I, I think this *(pause)* uh, tension of the menopause was, uh, dramatically brought into my conscious . . . I, I faced the fact that my brother, John, who had been living in the home that my mother left in her will to my children, was . . . suspecting that I had ideas of taking the house myself . . . and this probably is factually true. There is some basis for my suspicion that he, having been married since my mother's death, wanted the home for himself. And, there were a couple of incidents at home that, that summer. We were only there a few days, in which he became very angry with me, and yelled, ah, about my raising of the children. But mainly, it was, I think, what he had on his mind. Some things he said were certainly said without his knowledge and . . . Sir?

THERAPIST: I was wondering how old your brother was.

(The therapist is having difficulty following the material as the patient rambles on and on. Is this a punishment for ignoring her earlier request? Her use of "Sir," especially in view of what she had said about the "adjustment of the non-white to the white research group" is diagnostic. The patient obviously is repressing a great rage, with a reaction-formation of radiant politeness. We would

126

expect a passive-aggressive response from her to any inferior or deficient therapeutic communications.)

PATIENT: He's three years older than I; I'm forty-one.

THERAPIST: You're forty-one? He's forty-four?

PATIENT: Yes. Yes, he'll be forty-four in May. And uh, he, he's the older brother and he's the brother that we, we center all our affections on him. The other brother is the baby boy. He's three years younger than I. And since our father's death, he has been being the man of the family. And there are two girls, and we've leaned on him since adolescence, but this revelation, this uh . . . not revelation, this discovery that he was becoming not frank with me, but rather devious in his financial affairs. For example, he was purchasing a home, uh, for himself and, and it was a great secret. We've never had secrets between us. He had joined a secret society, and uh, seemed to resent my uh, innocent knowledge of the affair. At any rate, the . . . the seeming loss of a dear brother to me, upset me. Uh, emotionally. I began to forget things at that point. I'd forget where I put the baby's diapers; I'd forget where I lay a cigarette down. I would light two at once. I became a hazard to myself. I told my husband I had to get away. We returned immediately to Maywood where I got a good week's rest.

THERAPIST: This was the summer of '55, you say?

PATIENT: '56.

THERAPIST: Oh, '56.

PATIENT: '55, we made a pleasant trip.

THERAPIST: I see.

PATIENT: Now I have to get my years straight. '55, we made a pleasant trip to visit some former students of ours in Baltimore, my dentist, we visited my husband's relatives, who are of a large family and all of them older than he — many of whom we hadn't seen in five or six years. Philadelphia, Baltimore, Portsmouth, Virginia, but the summer of '56 — now I think I have the year right — is the summer that, with my brother, uh, I became upset.

THERAPIST: And you were pregnant at this time, also?

PATIENT: No. The baby had been born. I became pregnant in '55.

THERAPIST: I see.

PATIENT: I'm confused. The baby had been born in '56, March. And was at that time about four months old, And, uh . . . this is coincidence: The baby was born on the anniversary of my mother's death, seven years before, and was named for my mother, which is also my name.

THERAPIST: Namely?

PATIENT: Lela, yes. So that this little baby, to me, was very precious — and to all the family was — but we were upsetting her life. She had nothing to do with this clash of opinion. My brother, uh, when we returned to Maywood, was very apologetic. He called me long distance. He wrote several letters. He berated himself for ever making me upset because he realized I was pretty sick when I left there. But the week's rest did me a lot of good, and my husband was able to take a trip to Atlantic City to the A.C.S. convention. I was able to get the children all ready for school; the summer ended beautifully. And uh, during the, the school year, whereas I knew that I was a little bit in need of estrogens, I was taking the pills prescribed by Dr. Goff, uh, under whose care the baby had been born . . .

THERAPIST: It was estrogen you were taking? Estrogen pills?

(Out of frustration, the therapist reverts here to the "medical model." Again and again his brief questions are attempts to pin down the history he is trying to get straight. There is real irony in the "I see" — "I'm confused" exchange before. Returning to the role of "doctor" in a situation where the patient is being frustrating is a typical mistake; carried to the extreme, the therapist would give up attempting psychotherapy and resort to somatic treatments.)

PATIENT: Yes, uh, I know the trade name, Premarin, and they were quite effective. I think he had given me the minimal dosage, but the symptoms of insomnia and uh, chills at night, throwing off cover, and uh, inability to remember where I laid the cigarette, disappeared and I was getting along beautifully.

THERAPIST: Did they disappear when you took this week's rest, or did they start disappearing after you started taking the estrogen?

PATIENT: Until the week's rest, I was taking the hormones.

THERAPIST: I see.

PATIENT: I had left them, left off taking them, while we took this trip to Canton, and I had gone to pieces, actually, emotionally. I remember the night before we left: I wasn't able to sleep a bit. I remembered that I had some of these pills in a white crocheted bag, and I got up, as if in a trance, and took one, although the usual dosage was two. And uh, my husband looked after us until we got back to Maywood. Then I phoned Dr. Goff and asked whether the prescription would be all right to continue. He recommended it. This, because I didn't understand that a type of bleeding occurs in the menopause . . . that's really not menstruation but is a fl — flooding, and these pills would stop it. I was afraid to take them without the doctor's advice, thinking that they would cause increased menstruation. But this is the . . . climax of the story. A few weeks ago the . . . there began in Maywood a, a program for urban renewal, ah, you know what it's all about. And I was accidentally recruited as a member of the citizen's committee to form the advisory group.

THERAPIST: Accidentally?

PATIENT: It, it makes a nice story. Shall I tell it to you?

THERAPIST: If you think it's important, certainly.

PATIENT: Well, it might have some bearing because of my inactivity in civic affairs up to this time. What with traveling from state to state I'd never become interested, become interested in politics and never having my roots anywhere except in Canton, Ohio, I'd never become involved in community affairs, although we had participated in the usual drives for charity and we had become very strong pillars of the church in Maywood. The lady across the street — a member of the League of Women Voters, to which I applied for membership some months before, ah, was sick — phoned me and told me there was a meeting down at city hall. The League of Women Voters would like to know what's happening because the meeting hadn't been publicized; there seemed no fore, no preparation beforehand, and she was sure that it concerned urban renewal; would I represent her since she was sick? So, I went down to city hall and there were a hundred and fifty people, more than a hundred — I can't number — gathered. There was a meeting that seemed, ah, pretty well cut and dried. And, ah, I opened my big mouth saying that I wasn't invited but I was very interested in urban renewal and, ah, I didn't think that they should be secretly meeting but we should have a public meeting of all interested citizens, and if there were something which we could all cooperate. And I went on and gave the usual speech for open, honest dealing, but I was, uh, a little bit behind the times, I think, because this group had already been organized to conduct a survey — the people were all willing to do this work, the survey was there in mimeographed copy. Furthermore, they were all Negroes. And uh, I dif — , didn't like for this whole secret business to be any rate, having this . . .

THERAPIST: The secretness of all this bothered you?

PATIENT: Ha — , it did, especially when I, I realized that some of the questions on the survey were very personal. Uh, your income, where you'd like to be moved, uh, if your house, not if, but when your house is torn down, uh, how many people lived in your basement. Uh, personal things like that I thought were better placed in the hands of professional workers and I said so. And I think every citizen should object if his neighbor investigates his affairs to that extent. So, the, the meeting broke up on a rather sour note because the coordinator was new to Maywood and had thought everything was set. I talked with him in his office a while about human relations and how to get along with people. I'd been a teacher and I thought I could guide him. Although he was an older man, he had no experience in his work and, as far as I know, had never lived in Maywood. So, stumbling into this secret meeting, and having talked with the director afterwards, uh, it rather fell on my shoulders to join him, and I enjoyed it very much.

THERAPIST: I see.

PATIENT: But in the working out with these people of plans for urban renewal, I found in so many points that my ideas of democratic efficiency were either covered up, ignored, or contradicted that . . .

THERAPIST: Does that somehow lead up to this climax you were talking about?

PATIENT: This is the climax. That I was dealing in a problem of housing.

THERAPIST: I see.

PATIENT: And just a year before, I had, uh, found that in Canton, Ohio, this house actually — this symbolic security — was the thing that actually set off my suspicions about people's motives, and I, I, uh, longed for the time when this committee could start functioning and I could withdraw. The appointment of, uh, all members to the Maywood Committee, though, was a job that demanded a whole lot of weeding out because in this area in which we live, there are seven thousand Negroes crowded in an area where only two thousand should live.

THERAPIST: Now, was it this suspiciousness of people's motives that got you in the hospital?

(*From this flood of pseudo-medical and paranoid-sounding material, the therapist has correctly concluded that the patient has had a paranoid-schizophrenic episode recently, leading to her hospitalization. The therapist proceeds to question the patient about her past history, having satisfied himself about her present illness. He is also alert to the loaded word "climax"; words with significant double meaning should be carefully noted by the therapist, and it is sometimes a good interviewing technique to return them to the patient later, as illustrated above.*)

PATIENT: I rather think that was a, a precipitating cause, but I think, physiologically, I was in no condition to be worrying about two or three million dollars being spent on urban renewal. My own personal problem was one of trying to get a home that we liked in a location that we liked, and that was all wrapped up in this urban renewal project.

THERAPIST: Now, you speak of this going home to Ohio as having something to do with symbolic security. I wonder what you mean by that?

PATIENT: Well, home is, is . . . home in my family is maybe a little bit different from — you're younger than I — than the younger generation. It's a place where a mother and father and children, ah, form a tight little island secure against the whole world, and that's what it has been, has been to me, since I was born. And, ah, renewal, or urban renewal is picking up of people, relocating them or, ah, changing the . . .

THERAPIST: Separation?

PATIENT: That's right. Ah, it may be a fantasy but the idea of home and parents and family to me is an integral part of my personality, and getting involved in the dissolution of these things was wrong for me. I should never have opened my big mouth. But, I didn't see at the time that . . .

THERAPIST: Can you tell me something about your home and your parents and your family?

PATIENT: Sure, if I may smoke for a minute.

(This was another poor move with ominous overtones. The therapist interrupts the patient for no reason except his eagerness to get historical details, and the patient responds in terms of striking a bargain. Has the patient now concluded something about the therapist's deficiencies? Her second sentence below, beginning with "You have . . ." deserves careful attention.)

THERAPIST: Surely.

PATIENT: (*Pause*) May I have the ash tray? You have air conditioned offices here, and the currents that we don't know about are very effective. Well . . . there's so much to tell. My father was, ah, quite a man. He had been a minister in the South before he met and married my mother. Ah, both had been married before so they were older parents. And, ah, his education was only so far as a small theological seminary, probably the equivalent of the tenth grade nowadays. He was born in '71. In his day that was quite a good deal of education, but in addition to having, ah, great native intelligence, he had a wonderful voice and an avid desire to read. My mother, ah, she was to all intents and purposes, white; my father was about half-and-half, red and black . . . Ah, they decided when we were, ah, when I was less than three years old that the South was no place to raise children, so they packed four of us . . . No, first my father came to Canton, Ohio, and gave up his desire for the ministry and took a job in a steel mill.

THERAPIST: Before, we . . . you mentioned that your father was dark but your mother was white. Is that right?

PATIENT: Yes. She was raised as a colored woman. You know the type — like, ah, ah, Mr. White, the . . .

THERAPIST: Yes.

PATIENT: That type of Negro, she was . . .

THERAPIST: And you have some Indian blood in you?

PATIENT: On my father's side. His father was a Cherokee Indian . . .

THERAPIST: I see.

PATIENT: . . . and that's where we got the name Green. My father dropped the "Green Twig" and that's why we spell it without the "e." We were the Green family.

THERAPIST: Oh, I see. Your father dropped the "Green . . . "

PATIENT: The "Twig."

THERAPIST: Which was the . . .

PATIENT: His name was "Green Twig."

THERAPIST: Oh, I see.

PATIENT: So he was; his mother named him after the president, Zachary Taylor Green. So, we were no longer Indians because the Cherokees were shipped out to the reservation, you know, during the year — I wasn't there, I don't know. At any rate . . .

THERAPIST: So, the Cherokees were moved away from their . . .

PATIENT: Yeah, from around Florida, Georgia, Mississippi, up the coast to South Carolina . . .

THERAPIST: I see.

PATIENT: There were Creeks and Cherokees . . . first cousins.

THERAPIST: And how old were you when your father decided to leave the South?

PATIENT: Almost four years old. My father and my mother. My mother was quite a woman, too.

THERAPIST: I see.

PATIENT: They decided . . .

THERAPIST: This was after the birth of your brother?

PATIENT: After the birth of my baby brother. He was, ah, the "babe in arms," then there came me, then my brother, Johnny, then my older sister, Ruby, too.

THERAPIST: I see.

PATIENT: A girl and a boy . . .

THERAPIST: Right.

PATIENT: A girl and a boy. So, my father left the South where he, I think, he had quite a, a deal of prestige and could get along economically well. He left the South, came to Canton, and took a job in a steel mill. You, — in those days, — they worked twelve hours a day, six days a week. He worked until he had enough money to bring his family, and he brought, my mother brought us North. I remember the, the Mississippi, — no, the Ohio River we crossed. The name Cincinnati, uh, is associated with that trip. Also my mother's care, in seeing that we sat properly, that we had enough to eat. But Cincinnati marked our exodus from the South.

THERAPIST: It sounds like Mother was kind of strict.

PATIENT: She had to be. She had four children and she had to have some system, and uh, I don't think we ever would have made it six blocks if she hadn't — if ah she hadn't some type of organization — if we hadn't respect for her authority. At any rate, we came North at that early age specifically because I think my mother's and my father's ideas for us were a little bit beyond what we could have attained in the South. We lived, uh, on Vickstine Court. Uh, we went to Liberty School. The population then was about, in this school there were about five hundred children — Czechoslovakian, Hungarian, Jewish, Greek, uh, any Latin-European, there were no Swedes or English children. We were the Americans, the Greens.

THERAPIST: Well, now, as you remember your parents at that time, what kind of a person was your father?

PATIENT: Well, perhaps I could state it better this way. We never heard our mother call him anything except Mr. Green. We never heard her call him anything except pet.

THERAPIST: Was that a nickname, or . . .

PATIENT: Pet was a nickname. Oh, he was a, a man who read widely, who, uh, thought, I think, more deeply than any of us realized, who turned over his paycheck to our mother at the end of the week, yet, uh, she didn't spend money without his knowing it. Who provided to the best of his ability for all of us. Who had Sunday prayer and saw that all of us got to church on Sundays, and if there were some bad boys around, and there usually were, by the time he came home in the evening, we were ready for our punishment.

THERAPIST: He did the punishing?

PATIENT: Of the boys . . .

THERAPIST: Of the boys?

PATIENT: Yeah, uh, he never spanked either me or my sister. One time — and I know that this was wrong because my mother and I often talked about it later — one time, he did punish my sister, Ruby. And, I know that afterwards my mother said, "Mr. Green, That was wrong." But he never put his hand on us. He never spoke harshly to the girls. The boys were typical American boys and they were always in trouble. We were always fighting, but Mom would settle things if it's in the day-time, and we got — like I hit my brother with a rock one day and knocked the corner of his tooth off, or one time we got in a scrap over who should dry the dishes and my sister and I sort of tore into each other — and Mom would take care of those things. He was ah, ah, a God-fearing man, ah, and I think that he taught us to rely on God. Um, I remember very early that he would sing to us, ah, when we'd ask him in the evening. But, his job was to earn a living to, ah, raise a family, and there wasn't this "play on the floor business" with my father.

THERAPIST: What about the singing?

PATIENT: Ah, the singing was mostly church songs and he did enjoy singing them, and I remember early he would teach us many of the songs. Ah, in the old days, Christmas carols were not used in the South, certainly not among the Negro population, but in the North, when we began to go to school and learn Christmas carols, he taught us "Joy to the World," all five verses of it, which he remembered by heart. It was in his, in his, ah, church songbook, and he could sing that song very beautifully, and it was from one of his church books that I learned to read notes. Ah, I could follow the music and the words, and I got a little bit of teaching in school about the f-a-c-e and e-g-b-d-f and the names — do, re, me, fa, sol, la, ti, do — and the half notes, and I could actually teach myself a song from his, ah, hymnbook.

THERAPIST: Well, was he actually — down South — a minister?

PATIENT: He was an ordained Methodist-Episcopal minister.

THERAPIST: I see.

PATIENT: Ah, when he came North he found that there was in Canton a Methodist-Episcopal Church, but it was in the very northwest part of town, not among the poor. Ah, after the war there were immigrants to Canton by the thousands — ah, we were raised in that Italian community. There were a few Negroes there, but they were unfamiliar to me until I grew up to be about nine or ten years old. My father, however, did, ah, find that there was a, an A.M.E. church in Canton, and did found in Canton, while he was there, a little chapel — Turner's Chapel, which was given a sort of a charter by the Methodist Bish — Bishop in Cleveland, and that chapel, I think, is still in Canton and has had ministers succeeding him. Ah, on Sundays, that was, but he still . . .

THERAPIST: I see.

PATIENT: . . . he was a steel-working man for thirty years.

THERAPIST: And so, for thirty years after you moved . . . and you lived in Canton there . . .

PATIENT: All my life, yes, we lived there. Well, we went to this school where we had some exceptionally good teachers. Ah, they don't make them that way anymore. The type of teacher who can take a child who speaks Italian in the home, whose parents don't understand the, the, the language, and from the first grade up he's, he's learning day by day. I think I learned my English by having been tutored by these, these geniuses. They didn't play games with us except with the idea of teaching us something.

THERAPIST: You seem to have a lot of longing and respect for the past in your life.

(The patient is now presenting a long, complicated, and involved history. The therapist is thinking of the patient as "longing" for the breast, and this comment seems to hint in that direction. It is out of place here since the patient's enormous intellectual resistances must be dealt with first. The patient can be diagnosed as a borderline-schizophrenic who suffered a paranoid episode, now in remission, and who is typically bolstering herself with reaction-formation and intellectualization.[1] At any rate, she is in no condition to deal with early oral longings. It is the typical beginner's mistake to approach content without considering resistances. Predictably, she parries his approach with intellectualization, as beautifully illustrated below.)

PATIENT: I do. Ah, I think that that's not unique with me. If you will consider what's happened to our educational system in the past twenty years.

THERAPIST: Of course, the important thing here is to try to understand you.

PATIENT: Yeah.

THERAPIST: And you feel that this is important then, ah, this longing for the past that you have?

---

[1] Some readers may object and label her a paranoid-schizophrenic in remission. I prefer "borderline" because this was a single, brief episode, already over, and there are many intact neurotic defenses that have allowed her to accomplish quite a bit. The reader may take his choice since the points made in these interviews are not affected by the diagnosis.

PATIENT: No. I think you've, you've misunderstood me there. It's not longing for the past. It's an appreciation for those values that we had in the past . . .

THERAPIST: I see . . .

PATIENT: . . . that we are losing now. Values like discipline in the home that I've mentioned, respect for the head of the family that I mentioned, ah, a, a sort of respect for the ability of those teachers that I know is missing in my own children's environment. Those things, to me, ah, were priceless. Now, I don't regret losing them, but I do appreciate that we had at that time — something that very few families have nowadays.

THERAPIST: Your, two of your three children are in their teens now, isn't that right?

(So the therapist gives up and returns to history-taking. In making a dynamic appraisal of the patient, it is valuable to make one or two hints at the deeper dynamics in order to watch the patient's typical defensive systems in action.)

PATIENT: Yeah, yeah.

THERAPIST: And you imply that there isn't so much respect on their part as there was in your home?

PATIENT: I said their environment. I'm trying to teach them that I'm not quite crazy when I ask them to say "please" or to let me know when they go out, because so many of their companions don't.

THERAPIST: I see. Well, is it working?

PATIENT: Uh, I think so. Uh, the kids are very intelligent . . . a little bit. If they had been less isolated . . . see, I had them along in Arizona for, uh, three years . . . two years. When they learned to talk, they, uh, were in a Spanish community. The first thing they heard were Spanish words. The, the only person they knew was Mother and they were very close to me because of the travel. The army life was one in which you didn't set your roots down there. You only had one parent to cling to. And so, naturally, it was very easy for me to influence them one way or the other. Then, this college teaching that I did for about five years was another factor and on our side because we were in a community of college people and we weren't subjected to the, the town-gown of the big city life conflict.

THERAPIST: I see.

PATIENT: I think it's working. I don't know whether or not it's good for them or bad. It depends on what your standards are. I left out also the, the fact that in '48 — not '48 — '49, the year of my mother's death, I felt so desolate. I talked for months with a favorite priest in Canton and also with Father Schumacher, where I was teaching, and came back to Canton within about six to nine months after my mother's death. I accepted the Catholic religion and the children have been raised as Catholics. My husband became a Catholic a few years ago.

THERAPIST: This was after your mother's death that you changed your religion?

PATIENT: In 1950. Not changed.

THERAPIST: All right. But . . .

PATIENT: Uh, it's involved. Uh, my father of course had raised us all as good Christians. But I had gone away to college. I had, uh, become sophisticated. I had found there was no need for religion in my life. I was too busy. I did sing in the college chapel choir; I did attend religious services, just as a matter of form, but I had lost that feeling after five or six years that I had of closeness to some religious faith. And I had no need for it until my mother died.

THERAPIST: I see.

PATIENT: And after my mother's death, I began, uh, feeling the need — not so much for myself — but I, I felt for a time that I was offering these children everything — economic security, a good education, nice friends, a good home, a little bank account — but what about their, their spiritual welfare? I was giving them nothing. And they'd come home with questions, as children did, and I couldn't feed them that sophisticated materialism that, that satisfied me — especially after the death of my mother.

THERAPIST: I see.

PATIENT: So, I, I found in, in the Catholic religion, uh, a very strong, uh, refuge? Is that a good word?

THERAPIST: You ask the question as if you expect some approval or disapproval of the words that you use.

(The therapist realizes that something is not quite right about the patient asking whether "refuge" is a "good" word. It is significant that the patient does not pick up his cue but simply jumps over it. Why does she do this? The answer will appear shortly although sometimes it takes many sessions to find out what is wrong.)

PATIENT: (*Laughs*) I call it a, a refuge, but it, uh . . . Bulwark — that's a good word. At least it, it gave me something around which I could orient myself, my life, and the raising of these children. It's been good for the family and I think it's kept us together. I think that, had it not been for that faith, that my older children would have been delinquents long before then. And I, myself, think . . .

THERAPIST: They would have broken loose, if it wasn't for this?

PATIENT: Easily.

THERAPIST: I see.

PATIENT: It's, it means something for a child to be told the, the same thing by his priest and his teachers, and his mother and his father and his friends who are in the parochial school.

THERAPIST: Now, can you describe your mother?

PATIENT: Have I given enough on my father?

THERAPIST: Well, what do you mean? Enough what?

(The therapist correctly guesses that the patient feels that psychotherapy is "all give and no get." The situation is infinitely complicated by the racial overtones — with the "white boss" expecting performance by the "slave." If her performance is "approved" she will receive privileges [food, O.T., liberty]; otherwise, she will get nothing. It is common knowledge that the paranoid mind jumps to such conclusions.)

PATIENT: Ah, one more thing I think should go into this. He attained in his work, at Republic Steel, I think a unique distinction. He formulated the grease that was used in the factory there and, off the record, was a, a, a respected man in Republic when he did finally have to retire. They kept him on the payroll when they didn't have to, for about a year, and, ah, on his death, I think he, he left behind many, many friends in industry. That's quite unusual for a minister. Ah, and Johnny followed him into the steel mill, this brother, the . . .

THERAPIST: The one with the house in Canton?

(This was the first really serious mistake in the initial interview. When the patient again jumped over the therapist's cue, he should not have permitted or encouraged it. The time has come for a definitive and firm but gentle interpretation of resistance, based on the material mentioned in the preceding two parenthetical notes. The whole psychotherapy will stand or fall on the patient's capacity to recognize this resistance.)

PATIENT: . . . older brother. Mmm, mmm — that's the one. But, his is a top-level job, not at all the twelve-hour, six-day affair. He's a union man . . .

THERAPIST: I see.

PATIENT: . . . and he manages very well. My mother was, ah *(pause)* very beautiful when she was young. She had blue eyes and long black hair, and they say that she used to dance very well — some of the old, old people who knew her. She had ah, no relations, no brothers or sisters; her mother died when she was very young, and, when she married my father, she had, ah, been married previously to a man named Chestnut, who deserted her, died, was divorced, or something. At any rate, she married my father and was, ah *(pause)* ah, a good wife. I, I never heard her object publicly to him; before the children they would never discuss anything that hinted that maybe they disagreed. She agreed with him publicly, no matter what. It was not until I was thirty years old that I found that once in a while Mr. Green was a little bit in error, like this business of spanking my sister. It wasn't until we were grown women that she mentioned that to us. They used to talk together long hours after we were in bed but, ah, just the two of them. Never, and this is what's wrong, sometimes, with my family, we have an open forum of problems, and there's nothing that Champ and I might discuss that the children haven't heard of. I regret that. It was not a wise thing to do. She was, ah, an efficient housekeeper. She could take care of four children very well. She had some art in sewing. Her eyes were good. As to her intellect, it was, ah, well, this will give you an example. She had about four years of formal schooling, but she was the only woman in the section in which we lived who read from cover to cover *Time* magazine. That was one of the big moments in my life when I gave her a subscription to *Time* magazine, and she did read it until her death. She read history and biography; she condemned the novel — that was bad for us. Ah, she condemned, ah, trashy music; ah, she didn't allow us to use any except the kindest words, ah, not just curse words were forbidden, but slang words that we didn't know the meaning of. She was very modest and, uh, she had a sense of humor. She had ideas of, of uh, of better education for all of us. I think one of her greatest satisfactions was the fact that two of us went to college. I don't think that she wanted me to get married because the idea of a woman spending many years getting an education and then getting married, to her, was a come-down. Most people in, in her society would feel that if a woman gets an education, marriage was really not good enough for her. She should do something famous. But I did get married, and I . . .

THERAPIST: Do something famous?

PATIENT: Yeah, like write a book or found a university — make a million dollars.

THERAPIST: And was it felt at the time that you had great possibilities of doing something famous?

PATIENT: Oh, yes. I was a, a, the valedictorian of grammar school, and of the class of almost a thousand, I was a valedictorian

142

there. I went through college on a scholarship — I went up to Radcliffe on a Rosenwald Fellowship. I, well this seems like boasting, but I had a pretty high I.Q., and my mother, I'm sure, at the time that I got married thought all this is wasted. But before she died, I'm sure she changed her opinion. Because, I was then, not just raising a family, I was teaching, and she had more or less accepted my husband as a son, and, uh, marriage was just the thing for me. She was very proud of these two children, and uh, she loved them to death. But she wouldn't interfere with my methods of raising the children. She . . .

THERAPIST: She loved them to death?

(The therapist allows the patient to go on and on, and then he complicates matters by picking up a dynamically charged phrase that can only increase resistance!)

PATIENT: That's just an expression. To pieces — she loved them very much. Uh *(pause)* yeah. That could be quite significant, couldn't it? Except that I use the expression "love people to death" all the time. In this case, it may be. No, she didn't smother them with love. She loved them. But, if I believed this was a day when children should be raised by the book, if I believed that they should not be rocked, she wouldn't rock them. If I believed, uh, according to the book that they should be fed on schedule, uh, she wouldn't uh . . .

THERAPIST: I see.

PATIENT: . . . interfere at all. Although she knew best; I know, since I have this third child. And you probably know, if you follow child-rearing fads and fancies, that it's good to rock them nowadays. It's good to feed them when they're hungry. But when my two little ones were born, uh, child raising was a cold, calculated, formulated affair, and I, being an educated woman, tried to do what the book said.

THERAPIST: And what about when you were little children — you and your brothers and sisters? Was it a cold, calculated business, or was there more rocking, and so on?

PATIENT: We, we were loved. We were rocked when we cried, and uh, we were fed when we were hungry, I'm sure, and we were not spoiled. We were beaten when we did wrong. And we knew exactly when we were doing wrong. There wasn't any guesswork about I'll ask Mama because Papa said no or maybe.

THERAPIST: I see.

PATIENT: They, uh, they let us know very early just what we could and could not do. And yet, we loved them, as much as is possible for a child to love the parents. We, we coupled that love with a great deal of respect for a man who could say "I will do this," and then he did it. And, I'm sure that my children found that when I said "I'll do this," I probably would, and maybe I would not very early. And today, my daughter tells me, "You didn't raise us right. You're starting too late now to tell me to do this." She's fifteen and we can talk together like that. But there wasn't any of that talk together with my mother and my father. Uh, they were the parents and we were the children, and when we got to be twenty-one, then, we could raise our own.

THERAPIST: I see. Then you feel that this was the proper thing that should have happened, and this other business of when you were raising your children was not the right thing?

(The therapist does not recognize that the patient is again parrying his repetition of her loaded phrase with intellectualizations about child raising. The interview has now escaped his control, and he is participating in the defensive systems of the patient.)

PATIENT: I know. You see, I have my own experience; I have this first generation of my children, and then I have Lela. Now Lela is growing up, uh, in an entirely different atmosphere from my teenagers, and she is flourishing on it. Furthermore, well, the other children did, too. But emotionally, they were wrecks by the time they were five years old because I didn't know what I wanted for them to do. I wanted to raise them by the book.

THERAPIST: **Yes.**

PATIENT: I didn't trust my own judgment. This little baby, uh . . . Mothers worry about demand feeding. A mother knows when a child is hungry. Some way or other, she knows when a child's in pain. And I can tell the difference between a baby's, uh, temperature without calling the doctor and bringing a thermometer. Just press his face, her face, against mine, gives me an idea whether she is fretful or not. So, it's not a question of . . . I think I've tried, and I've made all the mistakes possible.

THERAPIST: I see.

PATIENT: So, I, I should be a pretty good mother on this child. But, back to my mother. She was a forceful character. Once a, a school teacher punished me, uh, by mistake. I'm sure it was by mistake. She thought that I was the one who committed the crime, and she slapped me, and my nose bleeds very easily. And, when I went home, I had blood on the front of my dress. My mother went directly to the superintendent and, without screaming or yelling, she told the superintendent exactly what she should have done and exactly what she expected her to do. The next time she found one of her children doing wrong, she was, uh, I think, uh, in the capacity to do a whole lot of good for that school, but it never happened again. She didn't hesitate to stand up for something that she thought was right, and she didn't change convictions from one day to the other.

THERAPIST: Now, how does that compare with you? Some of that in you, too?

(Is this a feeble attempt to regain control?)

PATIENT: I'm afraid so.

THERAPIST: Would you say you're more like your mother or more like your father?

PATIENT: Oh, uh . . . I think I'm very much like my mother.

THERAPIST: More like your mother?

PATIENT: Yeah. I think that, uh, my brother John . . . was more like my father, but now that the younger boy is getting more mature and settled, I don't know which it is, but between the two of them there is a, the character of my father. Maybe the younger one, more in these years, than the older one.

THERAPIST: I see. Well, the time is up for today. We'll go on from here tomorrow morning.

(*No mention was made about anything for the patient, that is, O.T. privileges! The remainder of this interview is an absolute classic and should be studied carefully.*)

PATIENT: Could I ask you one question . . .

THERAPIST: Surely.

PATIENT: . . . since we have about one minute? Ah, can you tell me exactly whether there's something wrong with me?

THERAPIST: Why don't you start with that tomorrow? Okay?

PATIENT: Ohh, Doctor! Okay. You won't tell me, not even one word?

THERAPIST: We'll talk about it tomorrow.

PATIENT: Okay, Doctor. Thanks for your time.

Comments spoken by the therapist into the tape recorder immediately after the interview:

(*One or two sentences were lost because of some garbling on the tape.*) Mother, in that the mother goes to the superintendent and tells what she wants to be done and how she wants it done without raising her voice or showing any emotion. And I think that the basic problem in therapy with this woman is going to be getting her to really express her feelings and emotions. I think that she's willing to feed me with these intellectual explanations, and so on, and discussions — all that I want — but it will mean nothing to her in terms of therapy.

One of the most striking things about the hour was that she came in and started off the hour by asking for something. And this was something concrete. She wants to go to O.T. And that at the end of the hour I couldn't get rid of her. She wanted to cling to me. She wanted again to know about herself — that I should tell her something, that I should feed her. And I see this problem in therapy with this patient, not in terms of an intellectual exchange — getting all the history, and getting all the data, and so forth — but rather on an oral level. I think that this is a very deprived woman on a very oral level. She describes her mother as someone who made the children sit up, very strict, and brought them something to eat. The rest of the dynamics are obvious, I think, in the answers, and I won't go into that.

My own feeling about working with this patient is going to be in terms of: Can I penetrate this barrier that she puts up? One way of doing that, that I tried to do in the hour, was to pick up a couple of little remarks she made, such as "mother loving the children to death" or "them to pieces," and hoping that perhaps this will stimulate some emotional response. But, I did not feel that it did. The only time I thought she showed some emotion during the interview was when she became very defiant about how children should be raised. And there was some oscillation during the hour between asking for approval, in wanting to know what she should say and do, and being very defiant and controlling in telling me what she knew was the way to do things.

I think that's all.

(In these comments, the therapist reveals that he has a general grasp of the situation and gives some hints of why he allowed the interview to proceed as he did at the end. The therapist needs to "penetrate" through the defensive systems directly rather than to interpret them. This need is probably multiply determined, and one must be careful not to simply dismiss it as a neurotic hangup in the therapist. The determining factors could include: an oral-aggressive response in the therapist to the frustrating defensive system of the patient, the hidden powerful oral-aggressive drives of the patient, or both; the neophyte's need for fast results; the therapist's anxiety about his performance in front of his peers and supervisors; or the therapist's neurotic problems about "penetrating" women.

The main point is that a common beginner's error is being

made here: the attempt to do something actively, rather than to patiently interpret the defensive systems of the patient while establishing a therapeutic alliance over many sessions. It should be noted that the therapist has actually kept most of this active medical-model desire to do something in check during this first interview; his worst error was in not approaching the defensive systems by gentle interpretation — an error of omission.)

SECOND INTERVIEW

PATIENT: Thanks for O.T. privileges. And, for something else, too. Will my husband be able to visit me?

(What has happened? Has the therapist thought it over? Notice how, typically, the patient responds to the granting of one privilege with a request for another. Still, this opening is much healthier than the one during the first interview.)

THERAPIST: Please speak a little louder.

(See the first parenthetical note in the first interview.)

PATIENT: Will my husband be able to visit me? I was told I would have to ask your permission.
THERAPIST: Well, I have to take that up with the administration and then I will have to let you know.
PATIENT: Fine, fine.
THERAPIST: That isn't something that just depends on what I say.
PATIENT: I see. I'd like very much to see him.
THERAPIST: Well, since you started off with your husband this morning, why don't you tell me something about him? What kind of a person is he?

(This question misses the point. If the therapist wishes to pick up the patient's cue about seeing her husband, he should have tried to explore her feelings about seeing him. His present approach goes back to the "you-give-me-and-I'll-give-you" of the first interview.)

PATIENT : Well, in, uh, racial background, his is almost identical to mine.

THERAPIST : Oh, some Indian blood, too?

PATIENT : Yes, Cherokee Indian, uh, Irish white forebears, and on his father's side, also some Negro ancestry. His mother was of . . . his mother brought the Indian ancestry in with white ancestry. His father brought the Negro ancestry with a little bit of white, uh, parents. So, each of us is about fifty percent, twenty-five, twenty-five — as the races go. He comes of a very large family. There were twelve children in his family and a very long-lived family. His mother and father both lived beyond seventy-two years old, as mine did, and uh, a very religious family. His father was a pillar of the church and raised his children according to the Methodist teachings. They had about the same type of religious home as we had, but uh, with a large family, there were some black sheep in the family. Uh, all of the children are older than he; he was the baby of the family and, I think, treated as a baby too long. His mother adored him. Uh, of the children in the family, there were four who were college graduates, one who has been a sailor since 1918 and is still sailing. He got caught in this Suez closing of the Canal and most recently came back home by way of the, the South Africa round trip. He has now joined the sister who lives in Brooklyn. He has another sister who lives in Portsmouth and another sister who has a very high position as the wife of a general officer in the church, the editor of the *Christian Recorder,* and now the editor of the *Church Review.* So, he's a nationally known man, and some say that he has aspirations to become a bishop. I doubt it, however. He's a Harvard man, this brother-in-law. Uh, now, Champ — that's my husband — uh, as a child wanted always to be a chemist, and I met him at college in the chemistry laboratory where I was taking chemistry, more or less, as a premedical or preeducational subject. He was a major in chemistry. He's an, was an athlete of some merit — a track man, basketball, tennis, baseball, football — although he's sort of light weight for football; he was at the time about 147. Uh, my first meet-

ing with him was at, on a freshman debate team. He and I
were accidentally thrown together. I was . . .

THERAPIST: To debate with each other, or . . .

PATIENT: To debate against each other, of all things. But, uh, we
had to compare briefs before, and we had to time our speeches,
and we did, uh, a little bit of research on the problem for
debate.

THERAPIST: What was the the debate?

PATIENT: I've even forgotten the subject. You know, the usual
classroom subjects, "Resolved that unemployment insurance
should be enacted", or, during those years they, they, the
National Forensic League sent a topic for national debates.

THERAPIST: What was your impression of his personality at that
time? What kind of a person did you think he was when you
first met him?

PATIENT: Well, for one thing, uh, he was a very gay young man.
He could dance beautifully. I was clumsy at dancing. Uh, he
could sing; he was, uh, my idea of what a nice young man
should be, although I didn't know anything about him. I was
attracted first to him, uh, just on, on the face, he was clean-
cut young man who was working his way through college
behind the steam table in the dining hall. He seemed to have
a very keen sense of humor and to be alert in his studies.
Later, in the chemistry laboratory, I found, of course, that he
did have scientific interests that were very close to mine, and
a couple of years later we, when I got privileges for weekend
trips, I did visit in his home and met his mother and his father.
We spent . . .

THERAPIST: So, your original interests were intellectual?

PATIENT: I think so. They, the sustaining interests were intellectual.
The, the first impression was "boy meets girl." I didn't know
what kind of brain he had when I first saw him, but I heard
the other waitresses calling him Champ and, uh, we spoke, we
smiled, and then in debating, we just happened to have been
chosen by our teacher, and we got to know each other. So,
a physical attraction led to intellectual contact, we would say,
and that I enjoyed very much. We spent most of our time

with each other either talking about our families and our lessons or studying; we had privileges of using the blackboard and the math library and a small room. We could work out our mathematics problems on the board together; we did our lab experiments . . .

THERAPIST: You worked out your mathematics problems on the board together?

PATIENT: Yeah. Uh, we had the same math teacher, and uh, Professor Bodui was his name. And there were several solutions we had at that time — analytical geometry — and we would compare answers and probably present two or three different ways to solve a problem, and there were very few lessons that we didn't come up with very good answers in class.

THERAPIST: Now since you've been married, what more have you learned about his personality?

PATIENT: Oh, I learned a lot more since I've been married than I did in college. Uh, I hinted that he was spoiled. I've learned since I've been married that his mother, uh, actually placed the affection that she should have had for her husband on her son. I point to this instance when my first baby was born. I was at that time in Philadelphia. Uh, my husband had taken me to stay with his folks because my mother was ill. She had broken her wrist. She wasn't sick, but she was actually incapacitated. So, I stayed with the parents during the birth or after the (whistles) I had two children. After the birth of my first child . . .

THERAPIST: Three children, didn't you?

PATIENT: I have three now, but this is the era of two little Cokerns. You remember there were . . .

THERAPIST: Two little Cokerns.

PATIENT: Two little Cokerns and two big Cokerns. You do remember that my baby girl is so young now that I must learn to refer to a family of three. There were . . .

THERAPIST: I see.

PATIENT: . . . thirteen and a half years that we had to consider *ad interim*. So, when I speak of those years, the two little Cokerns were all we had. On the birth of the baby boy, I was in Philadelphia with the parents. And, uh, the baby girl was, of course, taken out by, by the grandmother Cokern, and uh, one of the, the shocking things I discovered was that the grand-mother took great pleasure in referring to my baby as her baby and Champ's baby. And, even in my presence, the baby was never identified as being Champ's and Lela's baby, but "my baby and Champie's baby." To me at the time, it was disturb-ing because I was the only one — the only outsider among twelve or thirteen Cokerns. I had married into the family and I had borne a baby into the family, but I was not a member of the family. To carry this incident a little further because it, it impressed me, the grandmother, uh, wanted me to teach the baby to call her "Mama," and what the baby was to call me was never brought up. Uh, I think I resented it at the time, but we never came to any, uh, open discussion of it because we, before the baby could talk, actually, we had gone west to Tucson. But this over-affection of the mother for the son was something I discovered long after I'd been married. Another thing I discovered was, uh, an intense, uh, dislike that seemed to be through the whole family for the father. It seemed that years ago, the father had, uh, taken the salaries of the older boys, uh, working on the old principle, I think, that a father actually is due the earnings of the children, and uh, while the boys were old enough to work, they turned over their money to the father. When the younger Cokerns grew up, they seem-ingly teamed up against Mr. C. I personally like Mr. C.

THERAPIST: There aren't very many people that you don't like, are there?

PATIENT: There have been some people that I have hated. Shall I name a few, or shall I continue with my husband?

(*It is clear that this interview is continuing in the same format as the last one, with the patient in control. To any historical question, she can produce answers in tedious detail. The questions are all the same to her.*)

THERAPIST: Well, what I would be most interested in at this point is to get some idea what kind of a guy your husband is.

PATIENT: Oh.

THERAPIST: See?

PATIENT: He's uh, uh (*pause*) he's two people in one. Two or three, maybe. One is the spoiled boy who wants somebody to take care of him. I'm that person — I'm his mother. Ah, I hope you won't hold this against me . . .

THERAPIST: Hold it against you?

PATIENT: . . . but, I mean for having analyzed, ah, his, his motives. I, I have the feeling that he looks on me as his mother. Ah, to take care of him the way Miss Ada used to take care of him. He's incapable of making a decision. I would like some ice cream, for example, and ah, I ask him to go and bring me some ice cream; but I must first tell him the flavor, I must tell him how much, I must tell him when to bring it, I must tell him to serve it to me.

THERAPIST: I see.

PATIENT: Ah, and after that there's not much fun in it. Once I told him . . .

THERAPIST: Takes all the sport away.

PATIENT: Yeah. Once I told him to bring me some Washington cherry ice cream or some black walnut. He brought both. Ah, this making of decisions has been my responsibility — not so much before the war because we didn't establish a home until 1951 — but the decisions have always been mine to make and, uh, even as to what the children should, ah, eat for supper. Another characteristic is the, the eating habit that in the Cokern family is a main characteristic. All the sisters are obese. And ah, some, if not all, of the arguments that my husband and I have had, have had some relationship to eating or food. Ah, the Cokerns are great eaters. They, me, food is something to sustain the body and that's all there is. I eat whatever, I ate whatever was prepared at home just because everybody else ate it; my mother cooked it and it was good. Desserts meant nothing more to me, except a Sunday treat. Ah, the food was sustaining — greens and vegetables, fruits and . . . candy we saw once in a while, but we were healthy. I had never had a doctor for anything. But with the Cokerns it seemed that food was, ah, a little bit more than just something to sustain the body. Ah, it was something that you pondered, debated, expected, consumed, and enjoyed in retrospect . . .

THERAPIST: Food was very important.

(In his past few remarks, the therapist is trying to "penetrate" directly through the patient's defenses. She responds with a verbal smoke screen, disguised as being cooperative.)

PATIENT: . . . and then . . . food was the, the be-all . . . And in my house, if I want to make Champie very happy, feed him something, ah, that he likes, some rice with possibly some kidney beans on top — huge quantities of it; some spaghetti, ah, with much flavoring; some, ah, roast beef, about so thick, with lots of gravy. All these things are fattening, you know. And, be sure to impress him with the amount of time and care that I've spent. He will make the remark that this tastes as if you really did put a lot of effort into it. *Ach du liebe!* Who, the food will taste as good whether I put the effort into it, or . . .

THERAPIST: Now, you said you had a lot of arguments with him about this, ah, apparently you disapprove of this . . .

PATIENT: Well, ah my . . . not about this, but somewhere food has entered into it. Ah, seemingly by accident, but ah, when for example, he's had a hard day at the laboratory and I know that he's not feeling well, he will, ah, be very hungry. Sooner or later the point will come out that I am not feeding him correctly; he's hungry, he's worked very hard, and ah, I haven't really served him the meal that I should. I've been home all day with nothing to do — that's funny, with nothing to do, he says — and really he can't eat this meal.

THERAPIST: So then he gets upset, or he's tired or overworked — he gets very hungry . . .

PATIENT: He gets hungry and I get blamed for something or other. I, I've grown to know that when he comes home after an argument or some upsetting research, or possibly his boss hasn't been so good to him, that something's going to be wrong, and it's mainly going to be his food. I recently convinced him the . . . I've convinced him that he was overweight. He weighed 147 to 150 for years, until he went overseas. When he came home he gained and gained and gained until he was 177, and I finally — he's an intelligent fellow — we talked over obesity and longevity with him, and told him how much I would like for him to live as long as I did because men do gain weight and it shortens their life; why not diet.

THERAPIST: Now, what happens with you when you get, ah, tired and irritable and nervous and have a hard day in the house? I take it that you don't get hungry.

PATIENT: No, I drink coffee.

THERAPIST: You drink coffee when you . . .

PATIENT: I smoke cigarettes. I read a little bit. And, ah, I, I try to keep composed — outwardly, at least.

THERAPIST: Yes. You try very hard to keep everything under control.

(This is more to the point. Apparently the therapist realized he was getting nowhere and saw that the patient was controlling the interview. So now he plans to call her attention to her controlling defenses. He is well rewarded by the following material, which should be studied carefully.)

PATIENT: Yes. Ah, sometimes I, I know I'm a bother to the children and to my husband when I am nervous, and sometimes surprisingly I receive, ah, a great deal of understanding. Sometimes, on the other hand, when I am seen to be irritable, then there's a contest in the house to see who can be more irritable than Mother. I can start things off at home very beautifully by saying, "Gee! It's a lovely day. I feel wonderful. How do you feel, Champ?" He has to say he feels wonderful because he's healthy. The children feel wonderful. But if, perchance, I say I'm tired or I have a headache, well, Champ has a stomachache, Nicky has a broken leg, Rickie has a bent back, but, ah, there's competition . . . .

THERAPIST: I wonder if that could explain why you started off the last hour telling me about a beautiful sunset . . .

PATIENT: It was a sunrise.

(This is an excellent comment, followed by a slip of the tongue! It reveals that the therapist has psychotherapeutic talent: he has kept in mind the unusual opening of the last interview, and now attempts to tie it in with the patient's dynamics. This could have been done by a more experienced therapist during the last third of the first interview. Is it too late? The slip of the tongue is inexplicable at this point. It would be a major error for the therapist to dwell upon it or for us to offer superficial interpretations of it, as is done so often when interviews are watched and taped.)

THERAPIST: Sunrise, yes. Did you have in mind, ah . . .

PATIENT: No! What I had in . . .

THERAPIST: . . . making it a pleasant hour?

PATIENT: I had no idea that I was coming up here for an interview. Actually I thought that the procedure would be, first, a complete medical examination, then you meet your doctor. Actually the, the cheeriness of my smile was due to the fact that we'd been down at this dull, damp, humid end of the corridor, behind locked doors, and this was the first time that I had actually seen the sunrise.

THERAPIST: I see.

PATIENT: And, ah, it, it was really beautiful. And when I came up I was cheered because I looked forward to O.T. privileges and to, well, talking to my doctor and hoping that we'd get along, and then I had been in this room the day before — just a moment or two — with Dr. B., and it is a beautiful room and it was a lovely day outside. But no, I wasn't in the old routine, and I didn't really, deliberately, do this at home; just, in retrospect, remember that when I'm feeling good, everybody feels good, but if I complain, I get no sympathy; I get competition. If I have a headache, well, Champ's has been aching for two days and I didn't know anything about it. Then that's very wrong, so . . .

THERAPIST: What's very wrong? I didn't quite . . .

PATIENT: . . . actually, for me not to know that he had a headache for two days.

THERAPIST: Why do you think that's very wrong?

(What has happened? The therapist has allowed the patient to put up another verbal smoke screen again. He does not vigorously pursue the discussion of control but meekly follows the patient off on a tangent — back to her home life, and then all over the place. What is wrong? Is the slip of the tongue any clue?)

PATIENT: I don't think that. I'm quoting the . . .

THERAPIST: Oh.

PATIENT: . . . the, ah, reception I would get if I said I had a headache. Well, he will tell me he has a headache for two days. Ohh, it's been terrible! And then, I will sympathize with his headache, and he has forgotten that I really had a headache.

THERAPIST: So that, instead of him sympathizing with you . . .

PATIENT: He points to his own . . .

THERAPIST: . . . he points to his own problems and expects you to sympathize with him?

PATIENT: Yes. And . . .

THERAPIST: I see.

PATIENT: . . . in sympathizing with him, then I forget, or I try to forget, that I had a headache. And I know he forgets that I was the one who brought the subject up. But the price of peace and happiness is that, I suppose. Ah, when he does have a headache and complains, I say, "Well, Champ, if you have a headache, you should take an aspirin. May I get an aspirin for you?" "Ohh, no." "Well, people who have headaches should take an aspirin." "Ohh, no." So, I must suffer his headache.

THERAPIST: Mmm, mmm. And, when you have a headache and complain . . .

PATIENT: When I have a headache . . .

THERAPIST: . . . then all he says is "I have a worse headache"?

PATIENT: Yeah. When I have a headache I usually go and get an aspirin and try to get rid of it. Ah . . .

THERAPIST: I see.

PATIENT: There's very little, ah, complaining I can get around — get away with. But, I have been accused of complaining. Ah, for example, if I did say I have a headache, and he didn't first reply that he has had one for two days, he would say, "You shouldn't complain like that. I work all day." But I've learned how to keep it peaceful. If he's had a headache, I'm very sympathetic. That makes him feel very good; he goes off to work very cheerful; he forgets that I have one; and I'm very fortunate in not being disabled, physically, most of the time.

THERAPIST: And who does the sympathizing with you?

PATIENT: *(Sighs)* My little daughter, once in a while, in recent years. She's a young lady now. She does have deep insight, I think, deeper than most youngsters would have into the relationship of her father and her mother, and she, too, tries to keep things peaceful around the house.

THERAPIST: She kind of sees your side of the picture.

PATIENT: I'm sure she does. Although we don't discuss it openly, I'm sure that, uh, she sees a lot more than the average child would.

THERAPIST: *(His reply was lost on the tape.)*

PATIENT: For example, she would go and get a hot-water bottle if I had a stomachache.

THERAPIST: She'd go and . . .

PATIENT: Why sure. And she would say, uh, "You let the floor go tonight; don't scrub the floor if you're tired." Uh, the other boy, well, he's a man's man. He's a boy — a typical boy. Uh, he's sympathetic, I know, but he, he's awkward and clumsy, and uh, he knows on the day that I don't feel well, but he doesn't know what to do about it. He and I get along very well. He reminds me of my younger brother, more and more, than the little boy Jonathan. And, uh, we have our arguments on theoretical things. He never gives in on an argument.

THERAPIST: Uh, there's a lot of Johns in this family. The older brother is John, and the younger brother is Jonathan, or . . .

PATIENT: Yes.

THERAPIST: I see. I'm just getting the facts straight here.

PATIENT: John is the one who is three years older than I.

THERAPIST: Yes.

PATIENT: Jonathan is the baby boy in the family.

THERAPIST: I see.

PATIENT: I told you my father was religious. Jonathan is a good, sound, biblical name. John, as a matter of fact, was the son of Zachary in the Bible.

THERAPIST: Oh, yes.

PATIENT: Zachary Green . . .

THERAPIST: Grandfather . . .

PATIENT: . . . was the father of John Green. I don't know whether he consciously thought of it. John is such a common name, but Zachary was the father of John the Baptist who preceded the, ah, coming of Christ, prophesying, crying in the wilderness, and things like that.

THERAPIST: Yes. Now, can you tell me some more about your husband? What kind of a person he is?

(This question almost implies that the discussion of control had never taken place and that the therapist doesn't really know what to say next. He seems to have lost any focus in the interview. Why? Can you guess?)

PATIENT: Gee! There's so much! When he's, on good days he's the best of the best of the best. He's thoughtful and kind and considerate. He, ah, on good days he talks with. . . . We have plans, we, ah, are together in how we want to raise the children. He's very helpful in anything that I want to do — this is on good days — ah, we can concoct, ah, most delightful dinners if we talk them over beforehand. And, it's pleasing to him . . .

THERAPIST: The two of you talk over in advance sometimes . . .

PATIENT: Oh, yes.

THERAPIST: What you're going to have to eat?

PATIENT: I say this in all candidness — what he's going to have to eat.

THERAPIST: You don't count?

PATIENT: It doesn't make any difference to me. I can't get excited about the thing, but he can get enthusiastic, so I join in with his enthusiasm and we plan a lovely meal; and if he enjoys it, then we all do because if Daddy is happy, everybody is happy . . . in our little family. I mean, that's more or less the password. That's . . .

THERAPIST: The password?

PATIENT: The password. Daddy's happy — we are all happy. Ah, about his intellectual pursuits, he's ah . . .

THERAPIST: I'm not interested in the intellectual pursuits. What I want to know is what kind of a person this fellow is.

PATIENT: No? Oh, okay. He loves to eat. He loves to sleep. Oh, boy, does he love to sleep . . .

THERAPIST: He likes the simple things in life?

PATIENT: He likes for me to wake him up in the morning, Doctor. He will not wake up by an alarm clock. Not once must I wake him up, but several times, and nicely. Uh, I've learned to do that gracefully and cheerfully. But sometimes, I stop to think, uh, maybe his mother used to wake him up, and this makes him happy to be waked up by a person rather than by a clock. But there were those years in the army, I know, in which he had to get up.

THERAPIST: And he could do it without being . . .

PATIENT: I'm sure he did. There were those years in the army in which he made his own bed, I'm sure. Uh, so . . .

THERAPIST: Sounds to me like you have some resentment against having to do all these things.

PATIENT: A resentment?

THERAPIST: Yeah.

PATIENT: I could resent it, if he deliberately did it. But I can't resent something that is not his fault. Uh, I resent his mother. But she's dead, and I'm sure that possibly the things that she did were not her fault. Uh, each one of us . . .

THERAPIST: Yes. Well, then, of course, we're not here to make judgments about whose fault things are.

PATIENT: Yeah. Yeah.

THERAPIST: But, nevertheless, you know, emotions come up. Feelings come up.

PATIENT: They do, but we, we have the power to think, uh, and if I catch myself resenting something without justification, uh, I'm not using my own power of reasoning. I can see that an ordinary, uh, situation that brought about resentment could be the fault of the guy but could also be the fault of his mother. He can't help it if he, uh, is still wanting to be mothered.

THERAPIST: And on top of that, a new baby that has to be mothered.

PATIENT: Yes! Now, that's another story, too.

THERAPIST: Umm, umm. Go ahead.

(In the last few interchanges we see the therapist casting about from theme to theme, trying to get the patient to show some feeling besides her cold intellectualizations. The various attempts fail, and the patient produces one story after another. The therapist allows this to go on and on.)

PATIENT: The, uh, new baby. I don't know whether, uh, this is imagination or not, but I think that, uh, he uh, gets a little bit too much satisfaction out of mothering the baby, more or less, as a, a young girl, a, a baby girl with her doll would place a moderate amount of affection on the doll, but when it goes to extremes, uh, it's something to be regretted. Sometimes, my husband gives me the impression of, uh, wanting to be the mother of the baby, not the father. That may be purely, uh, imagination, I don't know. However, it seems *(pause)* yeah, it seems I deliberately stopped him from giving the baby the bottle because I, I have a very definite idea that a baby's first attachment should be mother milk to baby, not father milk to baby. And, whereas I, I like for him to hold the baby and rock the baby, I don't think that the, the emotional response of loving the mother should so soon be, uh, a dual thing. This may contradict pediatricians who say that father should give the baby the bottle half the time and mother half the time.

THERAPIST: Theory, theory, theory. What about feelings?

(The therapist realizes he is being checkmated. Notice the patient's response again — it is all for the therapist, nothing for her.)

PATIENT: What do you want, uh, feelings? How do I feel about him giving the baby the bottle?

THERAPIST: Umm, umm, umm, umm.

PATIENT: Well, I think it's bad for him. And, uh, bad for the baby.

THERAPIST: How do you feel when he does that?

PATIENT: Well, of the physical burden of giving the baby the bottle, relieved; of the emotional harm that it might do him or the child, a little worried.

THERAPIST: I see.

PATIENT: But without bringing that to the, the, the fore, or without openly discussing it, uh, somehow I think, I arrange that I should give the baby the milk, that Daddy should play on the floor with the baby. That he should walk the baby and rock the baby, but that he shouldn't take the baby into bed with him. You see? But this is all done, uh, without argument or without any "You do this, I'll do that," but it's just . . .

THERAPIST: Kind of behind the scenes. You arrange it then?

PATIENT: Manipulating, shall we say, for the . . .

THERAPIST: I know.

PATIENT: . . . the good of the family.

THERAPIST: Yes.

PATIENT: I think I've seen, uh, enough of little children to know that they do attach the, the one who gives them the milk to the the mother. And I, I don't think I would want our little daughter to have the father in the mother's role. Ah . . .

THERAPIST: I see.

PATIENT: . . . there's a difference between being a mother and helping Mother. And, you might say, maybe, ah, I'm trying to . . .

THERAPIST: Well, now, you mentioned that when you see these feelings coming up within you, you think the thing through and you try to get things under control. Is that correct?

PATIENT: Ye-es.

162

THERAPIST: Are you successful all the time in doing this?

(Finally, the therapist returns rather abruptly to the control theme. However, again he lets it slip by, without referring to what is going on between the patient and the therapist in the interview.)

PATIENT: Oh, no! *(Laughs)* Now, wouldn't that be good if I were? Many times I've failed. Many times I've let my . . . May I smoke?
THERAPIST: Why, certainly.

(See the patient's "bargain" about smoking in the first interview. Then note the patient's discussion of smoking when she is tired, irritable, and nervous at the opening of the second interview. The patient must maintain rigid control — it keeps her from a paranoid breakdown. The paradox of therapy is that if her control is too rigid to even permit her to relate to a therapist, no therapy can take place. However, direct penetration or even assault on her control system might lead to another breakdown. Sometimes direct penetration is the only possible alternative, but obviously it should be avoided if possible. What is needed here is a gentle, focused chipping away at the patient's need for control and at her underlying fears, as well as some direct giving [of privileges, etc.] to establish a therapeutic alliance that will enable her to relax the controls.)

PATIENT: Many times I've let my emotions run away with the situation. For example, when I know that, that asking questions irritates my husband — when I know that I should keep quiet — in all justice I feel that I have a right to ask a question and to expect a reasonable answer. And many times I don't quite, ah, keep my emotions under control and I will say . . .
THERAPIST: For instance?
PATIENT: For instance, ah, "How did your day go at work?" I'll ask. Ah, "Oh, the usual day. Very busy." "Well, tell us what happened. Did you hear any interesting gossip? Did you run

any new reactions? Did you meet any interesting people? What's happening in the wide, wide laboratory?" "Well, ah, I didn't meet anybody. Nothing happened. I just had a busy day." By then I know he's not in the mood to be questioned and that I should keep my mouth shut, but I'll pursue the thing.

THERAPIST: Ah, you clench your fist when you say that.

PATIENT: Yeah, I'll pursue the thing to the, to the bitter end, knowing . . .

THERAPIST: To the bitter end?

PATIENT: Yeah. Knowing that I'm going to get in trouble. And, I'll say, "Well, did you see ah, ah — what's his name — Sam Davis?" or "Did you see Francis Taylor?" or "How's Stan's baby doing?" And then he'll say, "Don't ask so many questions. All you do is ask questions. I had a hard day and I'm hungry." By then, I'm in trouble because then I'll have to say, "But dinner's nice, this is lovely food you're eating, and it would be even nicer if you would tell me what happened today. I'd like to hear you talk," knowing all the time that that's irritating him instead of just silently eating. Well, sometimes I silently eat when he's in a mood like that. Those days, uh, things are under control. But when I persist in asking questions — when I know he doesn't want me to ask any questions, just let him eat — well, I'm acting contrary to reason. Because I don't like for him to get angry and . . .

THERAPIST: Now, you feel that when you persist in asking questions, then something is out of control? Is that right?

PATIENT: Umm, when I persist in asking questions, I know that I'm not promoting peace.

THERAPIST: Yes.

PATIENT: But, uh, harsh, uh, conflict.

THERAPIST: Yes.

PATIENT: I know that, and and yet I can't help insisting on the right to ask questions.

THERAPIST: Yes. Now why do you think that this is so important that it gets out of control? What it is that's getting out of control here? Do you have any ideas on that?

*(At long last the therapist brings the discussion back to their rela-
tionship. He is well rewarded by the discussion that follows because
the patient finally reveals her feelings.)*

PATIENT: Well, uh, for example, you know that the best way to get
your matches back is to say, "Lela, may I have the matches?"
You know me well enough to know that if you insist on grabbing the matches, I'll get angry. As an intelligent young man,
you want the matches, you should say, "Lela, may I have the
matches?" Also, as an intelligent young man, you know I
should give you your matches. I shouldn't be holding them.
Make your choice. If you want to fight, you grab the matches.
If you want a peaceful, uh, "Give me the matches, Lela,
please," I'll give you the matches.

THERAPIST: Now, what do you think that you should get out of
psychiatry?

*(Now the therapist is a "young man," not "sir" or "doctor." The
therapist could either pick up on this or on her feeling that he is
"grabbing" something from her — her perception of his "penetration"? However, perhaps because of time considerations, he moves
to the question of her motivation for treatment, correctly tied together with the control issue.)*

PATIENT: As a patient?

THERAPIST: Yeah. Should we have nice, peaceful, quiet discussions . . .

*(A remarkable answer by the patient is not picked up. The patient's
answer shows how very far apart the patient and therapist are from
each other. She thinks that she is a harassed, normal person who
was accidentally brought to the hospital and subjected to this
grabby, young white man.)*

PATIENT: Discussions?

THERAPIST: . . . of sunrise and "everything is pleasant and under control," or is there something else that you might be able to get out of psychiatry?

PATIENT: I don't think, Doctor, seriously, I don't think that the problems I have can be solved by psychiatry.

(She rejects both the therapist and psychiatry, perhaps forever.)

THERAPIST: Tell me about that. Just why?

PATIENT: I had no problems as a child. I think I was very fortunate in growing up as a healthy, well-adjusted, happy, tomboyish, intelligent young lady. The problems that I have now are not the problems that psychiatry can solve. For example, I should like to buy a, a home of my choice. You can't help me.

THERAPIST: Yes, that's right.

PATIENT: You mean, no, you cannot?

THERAPIST: Umm, umm, no, I cannot buy the home for you . . .

PATIENT: No, you cannot.

THERAPIST: . . . if that's what you mean.

PATIENT: Or even get for me the right to buy a home where I please.

THERAPIST: Yes.

PATIENT: Society says that people of certain races . . .

THERAPIST: Yes.

PATIENT: . . . must buy here and so forth.

THERAPIST: That's right.

PATIENT: To me, that's a problem that I must either adjust to or bat my brains out. Well, I have a problem of, uh, my daughter, uh, wanting to go out with boys. Problems of shall she ride in cars or shall she go to dances. Uh, those are problems that arise out of present-day society, and I don't think psychi — psychiatric treatment could help me solve that problem. The problem of my husband wanting to eat all the time and then be babied. I don't think psychiatary, uh, psychiatric treatment can help me solve that problem because to solve that, you've got to treat him, and me, and the children, or . . .

THERAPIST: Now, what about the fact that, uh, your feelings about these things sometimes get out of control? Do you think maybe psychiatry could help you with that?

PATIENT: I think it's good sometimes to, ah *(pause)* to act the way you feel rather than to act the way you know will bring about a happy, ah, peaceful situation. I think it's good sometimes for me to say to my husband, "You are absolutely wrong. Oatmeal is a baby's food. If you like oatmeal, well, go on, eat oatmeal." Then, most of the time though, if he wants a bowl of oatmeal . . .

THERAPIST: Yeah?

PATIENT: . . . I'll go and fix him a bowl of oatmeal.

THERAPIST: Do you think you have some difficulties in this business and at times not be able to control things, and at other times, ah, trying to keep things in that you think maybe should be let out?

PATIENT: I have difficulty, of recent months, I think I mentioned to you, ah, and I think they're purely physiological in basis. I know the reactions of, ah, excessive pituitary activity. I . . .

THERAPIST: You used such a high-class word there — I was wondering what you had in mind.

PATIENT: You're a medical doctor, aren't you?

(The therapist has played his one trump card — and lost. The only admission he obtained was [paradoxically] that she sometimes did not have complete control. This she attributes entirely to physiology, as is typical.)

THERAPIST: Mmm, mmm.

PATIENT: Well, I, I know enough chemistry to know just this much — that when the ovaries are slowing down in function, that all the glandular balances are upset. And, I know — just from reading and knowledge, observation of an artificial menopause — that, ah, this activity and insomnia, this, ah, almost rhythmic recurrence of old, ah, memories in poetry — these things are associated with a, a glandular upset. And I know that many of them can be treated with estrogens. I know this from my own experience and from my sister's experience some years ago. So that, at this time in my life, I know that the little problems that were small become magnified. But, I do hope that . . .

THERAPIST: But nevertheless they're problems.

PATIENT: For this time; they're not forever.

THERAPIST: Yeah.

PATIENT: They are for a phase . . .

THERAPIST: Well, how come you ended up in the hospital here? You remember that was the first question I asked you when . . .

PATIENT: Yeah, I wish someone would tell me.

THERAPIST: I see. Well, what led up to your being brought into a hospital?

PATIENT: I think I mentioned to you that I was engaged in this committee work . . .

THERAPIST: Yeah. You had some suspicions about people. Is that right?

PATIENT: Ah, yes. Ah, up until my working very closely with these people — and I never have in my life, until recently — I, I was, I suppose I still am, the idealistic type of person, trusts everybody, suspects no ulterior motives, and then I find that politics is uugh, that my neighbors are uugh!

THERAPIST: Uugh?

PATIENT: That, ah, actually . . .

THERAPIST: Yeah. Well, how did that get you in here?

PATIENT: I suppose my husband brought me in here. Don't you know?

THERAPIST: Well, no, I don't know. You haven't told me yet how you came here.

PATIENT: I think I told you that I was discharged from Cook, where my husband had taken me . . .

THERAPIST: Yes.

PATIENT: . . . on the arrival of my sister, about the sixteenth of February. I think that I myself told him at that time that I was just tired, I was forgetting things, I couldn't keep track of the, the intervals of feeding the baby. I began, at that time, to suspect that, that I was ah, sick. And I asked him to, ah, take whatever steps he thought necessary to help me. He called Dr. W., I know, and I know that I was given some medicine at home. I remember that he called my sister to come and help because the young baby was there, and my sister did come. But, how I ended in a psychiatric hospital, I don't know. As the books say, everything is a blank to me.

(The therapist now tries an extra-interview argument — the fact that she is indeed in the hospital. The patient simply denies it — an indication of her ominous mental state and the rigidity of her defenses. Her last sentence is classic!)

THERAPIST: Well, now, if, ah, you did end in a psychiatric hospital . . .

PATIENT: They keep saying, "You were very sick, Lela. This was an emergency. That's why you are here." But I, I don't know the emergency in itself. I asked my husband, "What did I do? Did I scream? Did I shout? Did I collapse?" And the only answer I get is, "You were very sick. This was an emergency." So I say, "Okay, I was very sick. But I feel fine. I feel better than I've ever felt in my life."

THERAPIST: Now, if you are in a psychiatric hospital, could that not indicate that maybe there are some people who think that your problems are not all glandular?

PATIENT: Yes. My husband?

THERAPIST: Well, whoever put you in Cook County and whoever transferred you over here must have had some feelings that maybe this is a psychiatric problem and not only a glandular problem.

PATIENT: Possibly so. I mean, I, I'll agree with that — not entirely a glandular problem. I don't think anyone can ignore the fact that treatments for the, the change of life have been, in my case, very effective up until a few weeks ago.

THERAPIST: Yes.

PATIENT: It would seem that . . . I don't know, I haven't seen my husband, uh, to talk about it. It simply would seem to me that the best place would be a medical hospital. But maybe I did, or said . . .

(Now the therapist pays the price for not having asked the patient earlier how she felt about seeing her husband. The entire interview has been conducted backwards! The patient is confused about what she is doing in the hospital and why all the restrictions have been put on her. She wants to talk to her husband about it; he isn't much, but he is all she really has to [ambivalently] relate to. Instead, she has to spend these two interviews producing what to her seems to be utterly irrelevant information in order to please the doctor so he will give her privileges.)

THERAPIST: But maybe it's not entirely a glandular . . .

PATIENT: I mean, it's, it's not at all clear to me what precipitated my admittance to Cook County.

THERAPIST: Yeah.

PATIENT: And maybe, one day, I'll find out what it was.

THERAPIST: Well, does this give you some feeling that maybe, ah, psychiatry has something to offer you also?

PATIENT: No, because I don't think that it's possible for my husband to judge whether I'm in need of psychiatric treatment or not.

THERAPIST: Umm. Well, of course, they would have discharged you from the hospital if they thought that your husband was wrong.

PATIENT: They did discharge me.

THERAPIST: Here you are. So, they discharged you from there and brought you over here. Is that what you mean?

PATIENT: They didn't bring me over here. He brought me.

THERAPIST: He brought you over here?

PATIENT: I came because I realized . . .

THERAPIST: And you were seen by a doctor when you were admitted here?

PATIENT: No.

THERAPIST: No doctor interviewed you at all?

PATIENT: No.

THERAPIST: I see.

PATIENT: I have been here four days, waiting for someone to tell me . . . and I will listen . . .

THERAPIST: I see.

PATIENT: Lela, you have such and such a complex; we are going to help you. But, everybody wants to help me with my problems, and what these problems are, I don't know. I've mentioned a few that I do have to you. There are many more, but they're certainly outside the realm of psychiatric aid.

THERAPIST: I see.

PATIENT: If, for example, I were like, ah, there's a patient downstairs who's catatonic. She has a problem. Psychiatry can help her. There is one down there who's depressed. You could help her. There's one one down there who's morbid about, ah, marriage. You could help her. Me, I don't know. I'm willing to be helped, believe me, but first we have to define the problem. Where do I need the help?

THERAPIST: Can you . . . Maybe that's what we ought to work on then, is to try to define the problem.

PATIENT: Well, you personally can do that, can you, can't you?

THERAPIST: Not without your help.

PATIENT: We can invent a problem, if we must, and then solve it.

THERAPIST: But you feel that, ah, there are problems. You brought these up yourself.

PATIENT: I mentioned those that I felt psychiatry could not help me in. I don't know of any problems that I have that psychiatry can help me in.

THERAPIST: Okay.

PATIENT: Therefore, that's why I say, if we must invent some problems, Doctor, let's invent some and solve them.

THERAPIST: I see.

PATIENT: Because physically, I, I'm feeling good. Emotionally, I, I feel very good, too. Uh, I can go out and face the problems that I left in Maywood with a great deal more calm than I could a few weeks ago. I think that's because I got a much needed rest, uh, from the family, and a rest with good food, lots of sleep, and the most loving attention anybody could ever have. I'm not even permitted to make a bed downstairs. But there's a point reached at which all this rest, uh, becomes just a little too much. I'm accustomed to physical activity. That's why

I came crying, "Can I go to O.T.? Please let me do something because I'm just sitting and reading and smoking cigarettes and being cheerful and . . . but I need something to do with my hands." Uh, you can understand that. All my life I've had something to do, something to play, some place to go, somebody to take care of. And here, I'm being taken care of. So it, it's pretty hard to adjust to it. But I'm trying to do so cheerfully because I know that if I can become physically strong, I can take better care of my little family. And emotionally strong. Uh, I'm just getting out of the scene of activity for a little while. Uh, well, that's that. Now, speaking of, uh, getting out of the scene a little while, is it good for me to read a lot while I'm here? I, I've been going through the library and reading *Time*, two issues, and all the *Life* magazines. (*Pause*) I'm tired of reading *Time*.

THERAPIST: Okay. Let's go on with this next Thursday.

PATIENT: Yes, Doctor.

(*It is clear from the final material that the patient's impression of the hospital and admission routines also has something to do with her rejection of psychiatry. It would, of course, have been much better if this could have been discussed, ventilated, and adjusted at the beginning of the first interview. When the therapist made a slip of the tongue about the sunset, he began to lose his way in this interview. Was he preoccupied with something?)*

Comments spoken by the therapist into the tape recorder at end of the interview.

First, I want to mention that there's one irregularity about this hour. There was a death in the family, yesterday, of someone who was close to me, and I was feeling extremely depressed. I did not sleep last night, and I don't know whether it came out in this hour or not, but I think it's an important fact.

Now about the material: Yesterday, when I started out, I began with an unstructured situation, allowing the patient to make the first remarks. And these remarks revolved around, first of all, a kind of ethereal, dreamlike, sunrise business, and uh, "Give me something." Or, as the patient put it today, "I came crying to you for something." As soon as the patient said this, I felt that here is someone who very likely is schizophrenic. Let's structure the situation to make her more comfortable. This I did and began a classical kind of history-taking. I concluded the last hour talking about (when I made my comments after the hour) her tremendous orality in the situation, in terms of feeding and being fed. This was almost amazingly brought out in today's hour with almost no effort on my part.

Now, the question that appears to me at this point is: What kind of therapy to do with this patient? The suspicion that I had at the end of the last hour, which was also borne out this hour, is that this patient had been a good deal sicker than she represented to herself in the events leading up to her coming up to the hospital; there was some kind of full-blown paranoid break. I think that's obvious by now. Now the patient seems to be restituting; she seems to be covering over the situation. She seems to be using intellectual defenses, some depressive defenses, some compulsive and controlling defenses in a general effort to keep everything stuffed back in. The core of the problem is again revolving around taking care of the baby, feeding the baby, giving milk to the baby and the husband — who is also a big baby, wanting the same thing — and her tremendous hostility and rage about this. The great needs of the patient for a home and security and so on are very obvious here, and explain the tremendous rage that she has when she has to give all to everyone else for the price of peace, as she puts it.

My feeling at this point is that I will have to explore further in a kind of middle way — between attempting very hard to pull out the material and feelings, which might precipitate another break, and being very supportive and covering up, which will not give us enough information and will not motivate her for further therapy if necessary. My guess is, at this point, that this patient is in some kind of remission now and actually could go home within another week and come in as an outpatient. And this is the idea that I would have if I mere treating this patient without the experimental situation. However, I'll have to see, in the next couple of interviews, what more material can be brought out. In order to do this, I will structure the next couple of interviews much less than I structured these to see just how much she brings out and how she handles it. That's all.

(The mystery of the therapist is revealed. The patient signed out of the hospital against medical advice that same day and went home with her husband. No follow-up was obtained because she refused to cooperate or return, even as an outpatient.)

These two initial interviews have been presented in detail, together with comments, in order to demonstrate how a therapist's lack of empathy can destroy a psychotherapy at the very beginning. Other factors contributing to this specific failure include the fact that the interviews were observed by peers and supervisors and were tape-recorded, the fact that the therapist lacked experience and that he was profoundly affected by a personal vicissitude in his life. The history given by the patient also illustrates the combination of social, cultural, and psychological circumstances that help to produce a borderline-schizophrenic condition. It is extremely important to approach such patients with empathy in order to get them to remain in treatment.

7

Final Considerations: Toward a Deeper Understanding of Psychotherapeutic Interaction

No one, of course, denies the existence of subjective factors in the analyst and of countertransference in itself; but there seems to exist an important difference between what is generally acknowledged in practice and the real state of affairs. The first distortion of truth in "the myth of the analytic situation" is that analysis is an interaction between a sick person and a healthy one. The truth is that it is an interaction between two personalities, in both of which the ego is under pressure from the id, the superego, and the external world; each personality has its internal and external dependencies, anxieties, and pathological defenses; each is also a child with his internal parents; and each of these whole personalities — that of the analysand and that of the analyst — responds to every event of the analytic situation. Besides these similarities between the personalities of the analyst and analysand, there also exist differences, and one of these is in "objectivity". . . . True objectivity is based upon a form of internal division that enables the analyst to make himself (his own countertransference and subjectivity) the object of his continuous observation and analysis. This position also enables him to be relatively "objective" towards the analysand.

H. Racker,
Transference and Counter-Transference

I set out to ask the question "Why do psychotherapists fail?" Or conversely, "How can one become an optimal psychotherapist?" In this final chapter I will try to place this discussion in perspective, by emphasizing that no amount of knowledge can substitute for the massive countertransference reactions that invariably take place when the therapist does not have much self-knowledge, and that innumerable courses and seminars are no substitute for the psychotherapist's own intensive psychotherapy.

I will also present the rudiments of a nonmathematical approach to the special situation of individual psychotherapy, in which various views that apparently conflict can be reconciled. This approach is somewhat analogous to the special theory of relativity. I do not believe that analogues to the general theory of relativity or to the unified field theory of Einstein can yet be developed in psychotherapy, but the purpose of a special theory analogue is to improve the orientation of the psychotherapist's education and keep its various aspects in perspective.

In trying to help the therapist present an optimal psychic field, we must deal first with the matter of countertransference. Obviously severe countertransference problems in the therapist can completely distort the psychic field he presents. *Countertransference* (Reich, 1951; Orr, 1954) represents fleeting manifestations in the psychotherapist of behavior, feeling, and fantasy in response to the transference and personality of the patient at a given time in therapy. *Countertransference structure* (Tower, 1956) is a consistent and relatively permanent aggregate of feelings, fantasies, and ways of reacting that develop in the therapist in response to the patient over a long period of psychotherapy. A *countertransference neurosis* (Racker, 1968) exists when the patient becomes more important to the therapist than anyone else in his life. This development is always neurotic except perhaps in the psychotherapy of certain chronic schizophrenics.

Countertransference interferes with psychotherapy when it produces anxiety, but careful scrutiny of one's countertransference is an important tool for understanding the patient. Similarly, a thorough understanding of the countertransference structure yields much valuable information. When the transference and the countertransference structure are inspected at length, we have the best understanding in psychodynamic terms of how psychotherapy has healed or failed in any given case.

Racker (1968) points out:

> Through the analyst's interpretations, the form he gives them, his voice, through every attitude he adopts towards the patient, the latter perceives (consciously or unconsciously) the psychological state he happens to be in. . . . Thus the countertransference, by affecting the analyst's understanding and behavior, influences the patient and especially his transference, that is to say, the process on which the transformation of his personality and object relations so largely depend.

Racker emphasizes the need to study all manifestations of countertransference and their influence on the therapeutic process, for this area has been largely ignored.

The therapist's ego and superego must both be brought to the highest possible state of functioning; therefore, in order to be successful, the therapist will require personal psychotherapy. For example, Ernst Ticho (Appelbaum, 1970) points out that a perfectionistic ego ideal in the analyst leads to unreasonable, perfectionistic demands upon his patients; they, in turn, will become discouraged by such implicit high standards. An even greater danger is posed by the therapist who becomes "disappointed in his work because it fails to fulfill magical fantasies, so he excessively seeks new parameters or abandons the field entirely. The 'professional superego' needs the support of teamwork, consultation and professional societies in order to sustain its authenticity."

A thorough self-understanding is obviously necessary in order for the psychotherapist to comprehend his own countertransference or countertransference structure, and for preventing a countertransference neurosis. Therefore, everyone who intends to practice uncovering psychotherapy should first undertake his own long-term, intensive, uncovering, psychoanalytically oriented psychotherapy. In many cases, if a full-blown transference neurosis develops, this will proceed into a psychoanalysis; in others it will not. A person's inability to develop a full-blown transference neurosis should not disqualify him from doing psychotherapy (this would be an unreasonably rigid criterion), and there are other social and economic reasons why we cannot require every psychotherapist to have a formal psychoanalysis.

Ideally we hope that every psychotherapist will achieve the maximum self-understanding and the highest level of personal maturity; this should be considered a major accomplishment and a prerequisite for doing psychotherapy (it is more important than a number of courses or seminars). The student's motivations for doing psychotherapy must be thoroughly explored and his maturity raised to a level where he functions adequately under supervision, as judged by the training committee.

How early in training should one begin personal psychotherapy? *Those students who wish primarily to do psychotherapy should be offered a different curriculum from those who wish to practice other aspects of psychiatry. The curriculum for the former should include more supervision of psychotherapy cases, more seminars emphasizing the humanities and abstract studies, more exposure to the arts, and an early and thorough personal intensive psychotherapy.*

In order to round out my proposed changes in the psychotherapist's education, I will conclude with the development of a special theory of psychotherapeutic interaction. The traditional models of psychoanalytic treatment have been discussed in a difficult and erudite paper by Szasz (1957). He speaks of the chess model of psychoanalytic treatment, first suggested by Freud (1913). It is common knowledge that the opening and ending moves in a chess game have been exhaustively analyzed, but the middle moves offer innumerable creative possibilities; only general guidelines can be taught, followed by careful analysis of the games of master players.

Szasz also points out that in chess *"each player influences the other continuously.* Thus the same player plays differently against different opponents even though he may have a persistent 'style' of his own." Szasz later explores the weaknesses of the medical model of psychoanalytic treatment. The goal of treatment, he feels, is the "establishment of a never-ending, ever-deepening *scientific attitude* in the patient towards those segments of his life which constitute the sphere of psychoanalysis." A scientific attitude, in this context, means a person's ability to differentiate between the possible and the real in understanding himself and his relationships with others. Szasz may leave his reader with the feeling that developing a theory of therapy is quite complex and that all models of the treatment process are inadequate.

Since new and more comprehensive theories of psychotherapeutic interaction are needed, I will outline what I call a special theory of psychotherapeutic interaction. Just as the special theory of relativity holds only for certain special situations (observers in uniform relative motion), I use the phrase "special theory" (maintaining the analogy to physics) because my theory also holds only for certain special situations, — individual psychotherapy, using the definitions, settings, and techniques presented in my earlier book (Chessick, 1969a). A second analogy to the special theory of relativity is that my theory can be reduced to Freudian psychodynamics for everyday use, if certain limitations are observed. My special theory of psychotherapeutic interaction is not mathematical, and at present it is not possible to produce analogies to either the general theory of relativity or the unified field theory. I hope that this new theory will be able to indicate that there is less difference among the various schools of psychotherapy than was previously believed and be able to provide a better theory of failure in psychotherapy by emphasizing hitherto unnoticed or unrelated factors. Haley's (1969) sarcastic paper, "The Art of Being a Failure as a Therapist," and Shepard and Lee's (1970) superficial book, *Games Analysts Play,* both discuss failures that can be better understood by the special theory. According to Haley, "What has been lacking in the field of therapy is a theory of failure."

Whitaker and Malone (1953) present a concept that they call "symbolic synchronization and complementary articulation"; it rests on a belief that in *all* psychotherapy both participants have therapist and patient vectors within them. Therapist vectors are responses to the needs of the immature part of the other person.

Usually the therapist's responses are therapist vector responses to the patient; at times, however, the patient will respond with therapist vector responses to the relatively small (we hope), residual, immature part of the therapist. Patient vectors are demands for the expression of feeling from the other person (comparable to the demands of a hungry child for a response from his parents). It follows that the patient will get well only if the therapist's patient vectors do not make excessive demands on the patient's therapist vectors!

Although Whitaker and Malone draw a contrast between the "gross pathological patient vectors of the immature therapist" and the minimal, residual patient vectors in the mature therapist, they point out that successful psychotherapy requires the therapist to bring along *both* his therapist and patient vectors and engage in a total participation with the patient. The therapist expands the frontiers of his own emotional growth through the therapy; if he refuses to participate totally in this fashion, the patient experiences a rejection and so there is a failure, although neither therapist nor patient may be aware of what has happened. Many experienced psychotherapists have been able to confirm this by pointing out that in each successful psychotherapy they experience some aspect of further emotional growth, ego integration, or maturation (often called "learning") from their patients.

A second aspect of psychotherapy is the problem of the psychotherapist being caught between the two cultures described by Snow (1963). Even if the psychotherapist is sensitive and conscientious about his work, he will still be criticized by scientists for not being scientific. Yet he will not be accepted by the artist because many aspects of his work are scientific and not creative. But, in order to be a successful psychotherapist, he should have substantial experience in the arts and humanities.

It is usually assumed that psychotherapy is in part an art because of our remaining ignorance about the field. This assumption implies that as we gain more knowledge or, more precisely, *scientific understanding* of psychology and psychotherapy, the practice of psychotherapy will become more and more scientific, thereby approaching the classical doctor-patient model in medicine.

I maintain that this generally held assumption is completely wrong and that it accounts for much of the confusion and acrimony within our field, as well as for unfair, invidious comparisons with other "more scientific" branches of medicine. This assumption is based on a misconception about the nature of knowledge — a misconception that has prevailed for centuries as a squabble between the proponents of science and the proponents of the humanities — the two cultures.

The views expressed by Snow (1963) and Bronowski (1959) have perpetuated this misconception. Snow says that scientists and humanists differ in terms of personality; he is somewhat biased in favor of scientists and against literary intellectuals. However, he implies that with time, understanding, and patience, the two cultures can become one. Bronowski is even more specific: he sees a profound likeness in the creative acts of the mind required in art and science and urges a synthesis of both in one kind of investigation.

Levi, on the other hand (1969, 1970), believes that the disagreements and differences between scientists and humanists are more profound. Science focuses on facts and basically relies upon

THE SCIENTIFIC CHAIN OF MEANING	THE HUMANISTIC COMPLEX
(the language of the understanding)	(the language of the imagination)
true and false propositions	reality and appearance
the problem of error	the problem of illusion
causality and scientific law	destiny and human purpose
prediction and chance	fate and fortune
fact, matter of fact	drama, the dramatic event
competition, biological growth	tragedy
the stasis or equilibrium of systems	peace

a formulation of the principles of causation. The humanities are dramatic, emotional, and oriented to human purposes in a manner that cannot be allowed by the impersonality and objectivity of science; "the avowed and willing anthropocentrism of the humanities is far removed from the neutral 'causation' of science." Scientists and humanists *think* differently and use different languages, as illustrated in the above table from Levi (1969).

There are thus *not one, but two maps of reality — "one sober, factual, claiming to be custodian of the literal truth, the other mythical, playful, but claiming to point the way to a deeper wisdom" — that compete for allegiance in the divided mind of every individual man.* Levi tries to base this on the philosophy of Kant, who distinguishes between two vital faculties of the mind.[1] The first of these, discussed in the *Critique of Pure Reason* may be called "cognitive understanding"; it deals with the analytic presuppositions of mathematics and physics, the principles behind scientific assertions, the rational presuppositions of the natural sciences, and the pure concepts of the understanding. The second of these, called "reproductive" in the *Critique of Pure Reason* but changed to "creative" and treated at greater length in the *Critique of Judgement*, deals with the dialectic of illusion, the heuristic fictions of the mind — in short, the creative imagination or, to use Levi's expression, the humanistic imagination (Levi's phrase em-

---

[1] It should be noted that Kant was quite vague on this entire matter and contradicted himself, as a careful reading of the *Prolegomena,* the *Critique of Pure Reason,* and the *Critique of Judgement* will demonstrate. For a detailed discussion, see Ewing (1967), who writes: "Kant also distinguishes between the synthesis of imagination and the synthesis of understanding. The latter seems to be a necessary presupposition of all judgments, but without it we could still have images, though we presumably could not make judgments about them and say: — they are images of a particular kind. But, since they always include more than what is given in sense at the moment, images themselves presuppose a synthesis, which Kant ascribes to the imagination. As to what this synthesis does and what would be left if we took away both the synthesis of understanding and the synthesis of imagination there are conflicting views among commentators, and it is very difficult to decide."

phasizes the anthropomorphism of the humanistic imagination).
*Thus, scientific understanding and humanistic imagination are
fundamentally different and are grounded in different nuclear
operations of the mind.* The need to construct chains of casual
explanations as well as the need to construct heuristic, often
dramatic and anthropomorphic, explanatory fictions are both
fundamental human cognitive needs. This was recognized by Niels
Bohr (Heisenberg, 1971), who distinguished among the languages
of religion, science, and art, and suggested that "we ought to look
upon these different forms as complementary descriptions which,
though they exclude one another, are needed to convey the rich
possibilities flowing from man's relationship with the central order."

The special theory of psychotherapeutic interaction is based
on the above discussion and begins with what I call the "fourfold
roots of psychotherapeutic interaction." Maps of the psychic fields
interacting between the therapist and the patient must be bilingual.
Each language selects a center for the psychic field of the therapist
and another for that of the patient. In the language of scientific
understanding, the therapist may be described in terms of his ego
operations, countertransference structure, therapist and patient
vectors, and training in therapeutic technique; the patient may be
described in terms of his ego operations, a genetic-dynamic formulation, structural theory, transference, and patient and therapist
vectors. A scientific understanding of the process of psychotherapy
would have to consider the steady mutual influencing throughout
psychotherapy — on both conscious and unconscious levels — of
the psychic fields of the therapist and the patient, using the des-
criptive terminology outlined above.

In the language of the humanistic imagination (dramatic,
emotional, and oriented to human purposes) the two psychic fields
may be described in terms of power strivings, security operations,
caring, being there, "I and Thou," encounter, or basic anxiety,
depending upon one's preferred school of psychotherapy or philosopher. So there are *and always will be* two fundamentally
different and competing ways of describing the interaction between
the psychic fields of the therapist and the patient in the process of
psychotherapy.

The special theory of psychotherapeutic interaction maintains that these two fundamentally different ways of describing the continuous mutual influence of the psychic fields of patient and therapist upon one another are both necessary and useful; they do *not* compete with respect to truth or falsehood but merely illustrate the basic human need to describe reality in two radically different ways. Freud, because of his unusually wide erudition, had a tendency to switch back and forth between these languages in order to present as immediate and complete a description of the clinical phenomena as he possibly could. Besides, his contemporary readers had a significantly broader background in the humanities than the average American physician does today. What happened, of course, is that the two languages became confused in the minds of his less erudite followers and even more in the minds of general readers, so that a number of problems I have elsewhere called "pseudo-problems" (Chessick, 1961) arose, leading to various animosities that still persist.

The special theory of psychotherapeutic interaction with its fourfold roots is outlined in the table on page 185.

Obviously, psychotherapists are most inclined to fail when all aspects of the psychotherapeutic interaction are not taken into account. The best insurance against failure would be the ability to describe the interaction in *both* languages and to visualize maps of both psychic fields. Because of the limits of our knowledge, we can sometimes explain success or failure in one language but not in the other. A failure that seems inexplicable from the point of view of scientific understanding can sometimes be explained in the language of humanistic imagination, and vice versa. A standard joke among interns, who sometimes treat the chart rather than the patient, because they are harassed by their superiors, is that although the electrolytes were maintained at normal levels and the fluid balance was correct, the patient died.

The urgency for training future psychotherapists in the humanities, in abstract studies, and in the arts as well as the usual "scientific" subjects has now been given a theoretical foundation. In order to do an optimal job, the psychotherapist must be familiar with both the language of scientific understanding and humanistic

FOURFOLD ROOTS OF PSYCHOTHERAPEUTIC INTERACTION

	Scientific Understanding	**Humanistic Imagination**
THERAPIST	Personality or ego systems Countertransference structure Therapist and patient vectors Conduct of therapist Interpretations based on genetic-dynamic formulation	I Authentic life (we hope); encounter Basic anxiety; capacity for empathy Will to power; security operations Caring; being there, presence
PATIENT	**mutually interacting with** Personality or ego systems Transference Patient and therapist vectors Therapeutic alliance Working through, resistances	**mutually interacting with** Thou (not "it," we hope) *Sorge;* being cast into the world Capacity for trust; need-fear dilemma Life style; career line Labor of love (Freud)

imagination, and he must be able to shift back and forth between the maps of the interacting psychic fields, so that what he misses on one map he will find on the other! The psychotherapist's deeper understanding of the interaction will surely improve the psychic field he offers the patient and sharpen his empathic perception. With two languages for interpretation, he can choose the appropriate one for a given situation, thereby increasing the effectiveness of his therapeutic communication. The following quotations from two psychoanalysts illustrate the use of each language:

> The defense against the transference and the defense transference arise during the first phase of analysis as a way of avoiding current anxieties about the patient-analyst relationship, the regressive pulls, and the developing transferences. The defense against the transference is a simple unit of defense. It is a response to the external stress of beginning the analysis and participating in the demands of the analytic process. The defense transference is a more complicated unit of defense. It may involve several aspects of conflict and defense as well as other ego manifestations. Habitual modes of character adaptation are brought into the analysis to defend against the experiencing of the more complex and more threatening transference neurosis. . . . Ultimately these defenses attempt to avoid re-experiencing earlier painful traumatic states. . . . Particularly severe and unyielding defenses against the transference and defense transferences may interfere with the treatment. Defense transference countertransference fits between patient and analyst may also lead to interminable analyses with reinforcement of character patterns rather than change [Daniels, 1969].

.   .   .

> The activity of the therapist is aimed at helping man to master the incessant whirlpool created by the clash of the constructive and destructive tendencies within him. If he can manage to escape the zone of conflict man is able in this way to escape the ambivalence which constitutes the most pernicious poison to his psyche, the major obstacle to the blossoming of the

forces of love within him. These forces of love are infinitely more powerful in man than he may guess, provided that they are no longer constantly opposed, used or destroyed by conflictual currents [Nacht, 1969].

I sincerely hope that the special theory of psychotherapeutic interaction will be useful in putting an end to the needless acrimony and personal animosities in our field, many of which have arisen from a false claim of truth, confusion about the method of science, and — perhaps most important — the narcissistic need to be an "important authority" rather than to understand scientifically *and* to identify humanistically with the patient.

Contrary to dire predictions, the field of psychotherapy stands on the threshold of a great new expansion, both in the group and individual treatment modalities. At such a critical time it is especially important to have guiding points in order to prevent certain ridiculous extremes (such as nude groups in swimming pools) that make us the laughing stock of the public and cast aspersions on many faithful and dedicated clinicians. The two basic guiding points are, first, a relentless demand for methodological purity and adherence to scientific principles, with a careful thinking through of all hypotheses and experimentations; second, a profound devotion to the rights of the patient as a precious individual who always deserves to be treated in a considerate and humane fashion.

We must always work in a spirit of humility and service, remembering how little we know and how easy it is to go wrong. Our attitude should always be like that described (and lived) by Jaspers (1969):

Our point of departure is man's relation to man, the individual's way of dealing with the individual. In our world, linked fellowship seems like the true reality. Communication leads to our brightest moments and lends weight to our life. My philosophizing owes its every content to people who have come close to me. I consider it true in so far as it aids communication. Man cannot place himself above man; he can approach only those he meets on the same level. He cannot teach them what to do, but together they can find out what they want and what they are. There can be solidarity in what must animate our existence if it is to turn into being.

Bibliography

Adler, M. (1965). *The conditions of philosophy*. New York: Atheneum.

Allan, D. F. (1952). *The philosophy of Aristotle*. London: Oxford University Press.

Allen, D. et al. (1958). Resistance to learnings. *Journal of Medical Education* 33:373-379.

Appelbaum, A. (1970). Transactions of the Topeka Psychoanalytic Society. *Bulletin of the Menninger Clinic* 34:257-260.

Aristotle (1941). *Basic works of Aristotle*. Edited by R. McKeon. New York: Random House.

Arlow, J., and Brenner, C. (1964). *Psychoanalytic concepts and the structural theory*. New York: International Universities Press.

Augustine, St. (1951). *Confessions*. Translated by Edward Pusey. New York: Pocket Books.

Ayer, A. (1952). *Language, truth and logic*. New York: Dover.

Ayer, A. (1956). *The problems of knowledge*. Edinburgh: Penguin Books.

Barrett, W. (1958). *Irrational man*. New York: Doubleday.

Bernard, C. (1949). *An introduction to the study of experimental medicine*. New York: Henry Schuman.

Blackham, H. (1952). *Six existentialist thinkers.* London: Routledge and Kegan Paul.

Blakney, R., ed. (1960). *An Immanuel Kant reader.* New York: Harper & Row.

Bleuler, E. (1950). *Dementia praecox or the group of schizophrenias.* New York: International Universities Press.

Booth, W., ed. (1967). *The knowledge most worth having.* Chicago: University of Chicago Press.

Born, M. (1968). *My life and my views.* New York: Scribner.

Brennan, J. (1967). *The meaning of philosophy.* New York: Harper & Row.

Bridgman, P. (1950). *The way things are.* New York: Viking Press.

Brock, W. (1968). *Existence and being.* Chicago: Regnery.

Brody, B., ed. (1970). *Moral rules and particular circumstances.* Englewood Cliffs, N. J.: Prentice-Hall.

Brody, E. (1969). Psychiatry's continuing identity crisis: confusion or growth? *Psychiatry Digest,* June.

Bronowski, J. (1959). *Science and human values.* New York: Harper & Row.

Buber, M. (1958). *I and thou.* 2nd ed. Translated by Ronald Smith. New York: Scribner.

Burtt, E. (1939). *The English philosophers from Bacon to Mill.* New York: Modern Library.

Camus, A. (1957). *The stranger.* Translated by Stuart Gilbert. New York: Knopf.

Cantor, N. (1969). *Western civilization its genesis and destiny.* Glenview, Ill.: Scott, Foresman.

Castell, A. (1963). *An introduction to modern philosophy.* New York: Macmillan.

Chessick, R. D. (1961). Some problems and pseudo-problems in psychiatry. *Psychiatric Quarterly* 35:711-719.

Chessick, R. D. (1968a). Books to begin the study of man. *American Journal of Psychotherapy* 22:102-105.

Chessick, R. D. (1968b). The "crucial dilemma" of the therapist in the psychotherapy of borderland patients. *American Journal of Psychotherapy* 22:655-666.

Chessick, R. D. (1969a). *How psychotherapy heals.* New York: Science House.

Chessick, R. D. (1969b). On the quality of the physician's life. *Illinois Medical Journal,* August.

Chessick, R. D. (1971a). The borderline patient. In *The American handbook of psychiatry,* edited by S. Arieti. Toronto: University of Toronto Press (new edition forthcoming).

Chessick, R. D. (1971b). The being of man and the howling of cayotes. *American Journal of Psychotherapy,* July.

Clark, K. (1969). *Civilisation.* New York: Harper & Row.

Collingwood, C. (1967). *An autobiography.* London: Oxford University Press.

Copleston, F. (1965). *A history of philosophy.* New York: Doubleday, Image Books.

Crombie, I. (1962). *An examination of Plato's doctrines.* London: Routledge and Kegan Paul.

Daniels, R. (1969). Some early manifestations of transference. *Journal of the American Psychoanalytic Association* 17:995-1014.

Descartes, R. (1945). *Meditations.* Translated by J. Veitch. La Salle, Ill.: Open Court.

Deutsch, F. (1957). A footnote to Freud's "Fragment of an analysis of a case hysteria." *Psychoanalytic Quarterly* 26:159-167.

Deutsch, H. (1965). *Neuroses and character types.* New York: International Universities Press.

Dworkin, C., ed. (1970). *Determinism, free will and moral responsibility.* Englewood Cliffs, N. J.: Prentice-Hall.

D'Zmura, T. (1964). The function of individual supervision. *International Psychiatry Clinics* 1:381-387.

Edwards, P. (1967). *Encyclopedia of philosophy.* New York: Macmillan.

Ehrenwald, J. (1936). *Psychotherapy: myth and method.* New York: Grune & Stratton.

Einstein, A. (1954). *Ideas and opinions.* New York: Crown.

Einstein, A., and Infeld, L. (1938). *The evolution of physics.* New York: Simon and Schuster.

Eissler, K. (1943). Limitations to the psychotherapy of schizophrenia. *Psychiatry* 6:381-391.

Ekstein, R., and Wallerstein, R. (1958). *The teaching and learning of psychotherapy.* New York: Basic Books.

Emch, M. (1955). The social context of supervision. *International Journal of Psycho-analysis* 36:298-300.

Escoll, P., and Wood, H. (1967). Perception in residency training. *American Journal of Psychiatry* 124:187-193.

Ewing, A. (1967). *A short commentary on Kant's Critique of Pure Reason.* Chicago: University of Chicago Press.

Farber, L. (1957). The William Alanson White Memorial Lectures by Martin Buber. *Psychiatry* 20:95-129.

Fenichel, O. (1945). *The psychoanalytic theory of neuroses.* New York: Norton.

Fleming, J., and Benedek, T. (1964). Supervision. *Psychoanalytic Quarterly* 33:71-96.

Fleming, J., and Benedek, T. (1966). *Psychoanalytic supervision.* New York: Grune & Stratton.

Fleming, W. (1968). *Arts and ideas.* New York: Holt, Rinehart & Winston.

Ford, E. (1963). Being and becoming a psychotherapist: the search for identity. *American Journal of Psychotherapy* 17:472-482.

Frank, P. (1947). *Einstein: his life and times.* New York: Knopf.

Freud, A. (1969). *Difficulties in the path of psychoanalysis.* New York: International Universities Press.

Freud, S. (1905). *Fragment of an analysis of a case of hysteria.* Standard Edition, vol. 7. London: Hogarth Press.

Freud, S. (1913). *On beginning the treatment.* Standard Edition, vol. 12. London: Hogarth Press.

Freud, S. (1925). *Negation.* Standard Edition, vol. 19. London: Hogarth Press.

Freud, S. (1937). *Analysis terminable and interminable.* Standard Edition, vol. 23. London: Hogarth Press.

Friedman, M. (1955). *Martin Buber, the life of dialogue.* Chicago: University of Chicago Press.

Fromm-Reichman, F. (1950). *Principles of intensive psychotherapy.* Chicago: University of Chicago Press.

Galbraith, J. (1958). *The affluent society.* New York: New American Library, Mentor Books.

Gaskill, H., and Norton, J. (1968). Observations on psychiatric residency training. *Archives of Psychiatry* 18:7-15.

Gauthier, D., ed. (1970). *Morality and rational self-interest.* Englewood Cliffs, N. J.: Prentice-Hall.

Gelven, M. (1970). *A commentary on Heidegger's "Being and time."* New York: Harper & Row, Torchbooks.

Gibbon, E. (1961). *Autobiography.* Edited by D. A. Saunders. New York: World Publishing Company, Meridian Books.

Gilman, R. (1971). The femlib case against Freud. *The New York Time Magazine.* January 31.

Greenson, R. (1965). The working alliance and the transference neurosis. *Psychoanalytic Quarterly* 34:155-181.

Greenson, R. (1967). *The technique and practice of psychoanalysis.* New York: International Universities Press.

Grene, M. (1957). *Heidegger.* London: Bowes & Bowes.

Grotjahn, M. (1949). The role of identification in psychiatric and psychoanalytic training. *Psychiatry* 12:141-151.

Grotjahn, M. (1955). Problems and techniques of supervision. *Psychiatry* 18:9-15.

Guiora, A. et al. (1967). The continuous case seminar. *Psychiatry* 30:44-59.

Haley, J. (1969). The art of being a failure as a therapist. *American Journal of Orthopsychiatry* 39:691-695.

Halleck, S., and Woods, S. (1962). Emotional problems of psychiatric residents. *Psychiatry* 25:339-346.

Halmos, P. (1966). *The faith of the counsellors.* New York: Schocken Books.

Hartmann, H. (1958). *Ego psychology and the problem of adaptation.* New York: International Universities Press.

Heidegger, M. (1962). *Being and time.* Translated by J. Macquarrie and E. Robinson. New York: Harper & Row.

Heisenberg, W. (1971). *Physics and beyond.* New York: Harper & Row.

Hoch, P. (1948). *Failures in psychiatric treatment.* New York: Grune & Stratton.

Hollingshead, A., and Redlich F. (1958). *Social class and mental illness,* New York: Wiley.

Husserl, E. (1964). *The idea of phenomenology.* Translated by W. P. Alston and G. Nakhnikian. New York: Humanities Press.

James, W. (1967). *Essays on faith and morals.* New York: World Publishing Company, Meridian Books.

Jaspers, K. (1964). *The nature of psychotherapy.* Chicago: University of Chicago Press.

Jaspers, K. (1969). *Philosophy.* Vol. 1. Translated by E. B. Ashton. Chicago: University of Chicago Press.

Joad, C. (1946). *Guide to philosophy.* New York: Dover.

Jones, E. (1953). *The life and work of Sigmund Freud.* Vol. 1. New York: Basic Books.

Jones, E. (1955). *The life and work of Sigmund Freud.* Vol. 2. New York: Basic Books.

Jones, W. T. (1969). *A history of western philosophy.* 2nd ed. 4 vols. New York: Harcourt Brace Jovanovitch.

Kant, I (1963). *Critique of pure reason.* Translated by F. M. Mueller. New York: Doubleday, Anchor Books.

Kaufmann, W. (1960). *From Shakespeare to existentialism.* New York: Doubleday, Anchor Books.

Kierkegaard, S. (1954). *Fear and trembling* and *Sickness unto death.* Translated by Walter Lowrie. New York: Doubleday, Anchor Books.

Kockelmans, J. (1967). *Phenomenology.* New York: Doubleday.

Kuhn, T. (1962). *The structure of scientific revolutions.* Chicago: University of Chicago Press.

Landesman, C. (1970). *The foundations of knowledge.* Englewood Cliffs, N.J.: Prentice-Hall.

Langer, S. (1951). *Philosophy in a new key.* Cambridge, Mass.: Harvard University Press.

Lehrer, A., and Lehrer, K., eds. (1970). *Theory of meaning.* Englewood Cliffs, N.J.: Prentice-Hall.

Levi, A. (1959). *Philosophy and the modern world.* Bloomington: Indiana University Press.

Levi, A. (1963). *The six great humanistic essays of John Stuart Mill*. New York: Washington Square Press.

Levi, A. (1969). *Literature, philosophy and the imagination*. Bloomington: Indiana University Press.

Levi, A. (1970). *The humanities today*. Bloomington: Indiana University Press.

McNeill, W. (1963). *The rise of the West*. Chicago: University of Chicago Press.

Malraux, A. (1953). *The voices of silence*. New York: Doubleday.

Manuel, F. (1968). *A portrait of Isaac Newton*. Cambridge, Mass.: Harvard University Press.

Margolis, J. (1968). *An introduction to philosophical inquiry*. New York: Knopf.

Mavrodes, G. ed. (1970). *The rationality of belief in God*. Englewood Cliffs, N.J.: Prentice-Hall.

May, R. (1958). *Existence*. New York: Basic Books.

Merklin, L., and Little, R. (1967). Beginning psychiatry training syndrome. *American Journal of Psychiatry* 124:193–197.

Mill, J. (1960). *Autobiography*. New York: Columbia University Press.

Mullahy, P. (1948). *Oedipus, myth and complex*. New York: Hermitage Press.

Munroe, H. (1955). *Schools of psychoanalytic thought*. New York: Dryden Press.

Nacht, S. (1962). Curative factors in psychoanalysis. *International Journal of Psycho-analysis* 43:206-211.

Nacht, S. (1969). Reflections on the evolution of psychoanalytic knowledge. *International Journal of Psycho-analysis* 50:597.

Naess, A. (1968). *Four modern philosophers*. Translated by A. Hannay. Chicago: University of Chicago Press.

Nicklin, G., and Branch C. (1969). Quality control in psychiatric residency training. Paper read at meeting of the American Psychiatric Association, May.

Nietzsche, F. (1968a). *Basic writings*. Translated by W. Kaufmann. New York: Modern Library.

Nietzsche, F. (1968b). Thus spoke Zarathustra. In *The portable Nietzsche*, edited by W. Kaufmann. New York: Viking Press.

196

Oates, W., ed. (1940). *The Stoic and epicurean philosophers.* New York: Modern Library.

O'Connor, D. (1964). *A critical history of western philosophy.* New York: Free Press.

Odier, C. (1956). *Anxiety and magic thinking.* New York: International Universities Press.

Ornstein, P. (1968). Sorcerer's apprentice: the initial phase of training and education in psychiatry. *Comprehensive Psychiatry* 9:293-315.

Orr, D. (1954). Transference and countertransference. *Journal of the American Psychoanalytic Association* 2:621-670.

Ortega y Gasset, J. (1961). *What is philosophy?* Translated by Mildred Adams. New York: Norton.

Pascal, B. (1958). *Pensées.* Translated by W. F. Trotter. New York: Dutton.

Passmore, J. (1957). *A hundred years of philosophy.* London: Duckworth.

Pater, W. (1959). *The renaissance.* New York: New American Library, Mentor Books.

Peterson, M. (1970). *Thomas Jefferson and the new nation.* New York: Oxford University Press.

Plato (1937). *Dialogues.* 2 vols. Edited by B. Jowett. New York: Random House.

Popper, K. (1965). *Conjectures and refutations.* New York: Basic Books.

Racker, H. (1968). *Transference and counter-transference.* New York: International Universities Press.

Reich, A. (1951). On countertransference. *International Journal of Psycho-analysis* 32:25-31.

Reich, C. (1970). *The greening of America.* New York: Random House.

Rosenbaum, M. (1963). Problems in supervision of psychiatric residents in psychotherapy. *Archives of Neurology and Psychiatry* 69:43-48.

Rosenthal, V. (1969). Each therapist creates psychotherapy in his own image. *Voices* 5:17.

Ross, W. D. (1963). *Aristotle.* New York: World Publishing Company, Meridian Books.

Runes, D. (1957). *Spinoza — The road to inner freedom.* New York: Philosophical Library.

Russell, B. (1945). *A history of western philosophy.* New York: Simon and Schuster.

Russell, B. (1946). *The problems of philosophy.* London: Oxford University Press.

Russell, B. (1948). *Human knowledge.* New York: Simon and Schuster.

Russell, B. (1959a): *My philosophical development.* New York: Simon and Schuster.

Russell, B. (1959b). *Wisdom of the west.* New York: Doubleday.

Russell, B. (1961). *Basic writings.* New York: Simon and Schuster.

Russell, B. (1962). *In praise of idleness.* New York: Barnes & Noble.

Russell, B. (1968). *The conquest of happiness.* New York: Bantam Books.

Ryle, G. (1949). *The concept of mind.* New York: Barnes & Noble.

Sartre, J. P. (1964). *Nausea.* Translated by L. Alexander. New York: New Directions.

Saul, L. (1958). *The technic and practice of psychoanalysis.* Philadelphia: Lippincott.

Schafer, R. (1970). Heinz Hartmann's contributions to psychoanalysis. *International Journal of Psycho-analysis* 51:425-456.

Schaffer, J. (1968). *Philosophy of mind.* Englewood Cliffs, N.J.: Prentice-Hall.

Schilpp, P., ed. (1957). *The philosophy of Karl Jaspers.* New York: Tudor Publishing Co.

Schlessinger, N. (1966). Supervision of psychotherapy. *Archives of Psychiatry* 15:129-134.

Schmitt, R. (1969). *Martin Heidegger on being human.* New York: Random House.

Schopenhauer, A. (1958). *The world as will and representation.* 2 vols. Translated by E. F. Payne. New York: Dover.

Searles, H. (1955). The informational value of the supervisor's emotional experiences. *Psychiatry* 18:135-146.

Semrad, E. (1969). *Teaching psychotherapy of psychotic patients.* New York: Grune & Stratton.

Sharaf, M., and Levinson, D. (1964). The quest for omnipotence in professional training. *Psychiatry* 27:135-149.

Shepard, M., and Lee, M. (1970). *Games analysts play.* New York: Putnam.

Shorey, P. (1965). *What Plato said.* Chicago: University of Chicago Press.

Snow, C. P. (1963). *The two cultures.* New York: New American Library, Mentor Books.

Spiegel, J. (1956). Factors in the growth and development of the psychotherapist. *Journal of the American Psychoanalytic Association* 4:170-175.

Sprague, E. (1961). *What is philosophy?* New York: Oxford University Press.

Stafford-Clark, D. (1966). *What Freud really said.* New York: Schocken Books.

Staniforth, M. (1964). *Meditations of Marcus Aurelius.* Baltimore, Md.: Penguin Books.

Stone, L. (1961). *The psychoanalytic situation.* New York: International Universities Press.

Strupp, H. (1969). Toward a specification of teaching and learning in psychotherapy. *Archives of Psychiatry* 21:203-212.

Sullivan, J. (1952). *The limitations of science.* New York: New American Library, Mentor Books.

Szasz, T. (1957). On the theory of psychoanalytic treatment. *International Journal of Psycho-analysis* 38:166-182.

Tarachow, S. (1963). *An introduction to psychotherapy.* New York: International Universities Press.

Tischler, G. (1968). The beginning resident and supervision. *Archives of Psychiatry* 19:418-422.

Tolstoy, L. (1962). *What is art* and *Essays on art.* Translated by A. Maude. New York: Oxford University Press.

Tolstoy, L. (1965). *Anna Karenina.* Translated by C. Garnett. New York: Modern Library.

Tower, L. (1956). Countertransference. *Journal of the American Psychoanalytic Association* 4:224-255.

Voltaire (1949). *The portable Voltaire,* edited by B. R. Redman. Viking Press.

Wheelis, A. (1958). *The quest for identity.* New York: Norton.

Whitaker, C., and Malone, T. (1953). *The roots of psychotherapy.* Philadelphia: Blakiston.

Wiegert, E. (1970). *The courage to love.* New Haven: Yale University Press.

Wiener, P. (1953). *Readings in philosophy of science.* New York: Scribner.

Wittgenstein, L. (1953). *Philosophical investigations.* Translated by G. E. Anscombe. New York: Macmillan.

Wolberg, L. (1967). *The technique of psychotherapy.* New York: Grune & Stratton.

Wolberg, L., and Kildahl, J. (1970). *The dynamics of personality.* New York: Grune & Stratton.

Woods, J. et al. (1967). Basic psychiatric literature. *American Journal of Psychiatry* 124: 217-224.

Zilboorg, G. (1941). *A history of medical psychology.* New York: Norton.

INDEX

Free will, 62
Freud, Anna, 92
Freud, Sigmund, 21, 23, 24, 31, 33, 35, 45, 48, 56, 65, 66, 102, 103, 178, 184
Friedman, M., 26
Fromm, Erich, 23, 24
Fromm-Reichmann, Frieda, 121

Galileo, 20
Games Analysts Play (Shepard and Lee), 179
Gaskill, H., 74
Gauthier, D., 65
Gibbon, E., 49
Greenson, R., 85, 97, 98, 115, 118
Grene, M., 26
Grotjahn, M., 71, 75, 80

Haley, J., 179
Halleck, S., 73
Halmos, P., 84
Hartmann, H., 30
Heidegger, Martin, 25, 26, 31, 60, 61, 62
Heisenberg, W., 28, 31
Hertz, H., 22
Hoch, P., 92
Horney, Karen, 23, 24
Hume, David, 63
Husserl, Edmund, 25

I and Thou (Buber), 27
Identity crisis, of patient, 73
Interaction, psychotherapeutic, 175-188

Janet, Paul, 21
Jaspers, Karl, 18, 19, 26, 27, 31, 33, 187
Jefferson, Thomas, 56
Joad, C., 55
Jones, Ernest, 56, 103

Kant, Immanuel, 58, 63, 182
Kaufmann, W., 25
Kierkegaard, Sören, 25, 26, 30, 62

Kockelmans, J., 25
Kuhn, T., 45

Lee, Marjorie, 179
Levi, A., 181, 182
Levinson, D., 78
Lewis, Aubrey, 119, 120
Liebault, A. A., 21
Life style, concept of, 24
Logical positivism, 57

Mach, Ernst, 22, 27
Malone, T., 179, 180
Malraux, André, 48, 66
Marcel, G., 26
Margolis, J., 55
Maxwell, James C., 22, 28, 34
May, R., 27
Mental functioning, structural theory of, 21
Mental illness, 36
Metaphysics, 59-63
Mill, John Stuart, 56
Morality, concepts of, 64
Mullahy, P., 24
Munroe, H., 24

Nacht, S., 35
Naess, A., 26
Neurosis
    of abandonment, 107, 108, 109, 110, 112
    transference of, 176
Newton, Isaac, 20, 28, 33
Nietzsche, Friedrich, 25, 46, 48, 49, 50, 52, 62, 65, 66
Norton, J., 74

Odier, C., 107
Ontology, 61
Organismic conception, 20
Ornstein, P., 39, 74
Ortega y Gasset, José, 26, 49, 52

Pascal, Blaise, 25, 61, 62
Pater, W., 48, 66
Patient vectors, 180, 183

Peterson, M., 56
Phenomenology, 25, 30
Pinel, Philippe, 20
Pleasures, types of, 65
Poincaré, Henri, 22, 27
Positivism, 24
Principles of Intensive Psychotherapy (Fromm-Reichmann), 121
Problems and Techniques of Supervision (Grotjahn), 71
Psychoanalytic Theory of Neuroses, The (Fenichel), 113
Psychotherapy
  clinical studies of failure in, 91-121
  future of, 17-34
  neutral approach to, 19
  and philosophy, 49-69

Quantum theory, 28, 31

Racker, H., 175, 177
Reflections on the Evolution of Psychoanalytic Knowledge (Nacht), 35
Repetition compulsion, 24
Resident-supervisor relationship, 80-81
Resistance, patient, 97
Rosenbaum, M., 76, 82, 86
Rosenthal, V., 46
Russell, Bertrand, 19, 44, 53, 54, 55, 56, 63
Ryle, G., 62, 63

Sartre, Jean Paul, 26, 27, 62
Saul, L., 35
Schizophrenia, 31, 32
Schlesinger, N., 76
Schmitt, R., 26
Schopenhauer, Arthur, 48, 66
Searles, H., 76
Seminars, 81, 84-90
Semrad, E., 73, 74, 76, 80
Sharaf, M., 78
Shepard, Martin, 179
Signal theory of anxiety, 21

Snow, C. P., 181
Socioeconomic status, patient's quality of care and, 37
Socrates, 53
Spengler, Oswald, 56
Spiegel, J., 75
Sprague, E., 55
Stafford-Clark, D., 102
Structural theory of mental functioning, 21
Sullivan, Harry Stack, 23, 24
Supervision, psychiatric, 71-84, 89-90
Szasz, Tomas, 178, 179

Tarachow, S., 76
Technique of Psychotherapy, The (Wolberg), 45
Thucydides, 56
Ticho, Ernst, 177
Tillich, Paul, 26
Tischler, G., 79, 82
Tolstoy, Leo, 48, 63
Toynbee, Arnold, 56
Transference and Counter-Transference (Racker), 175
Transference neurosis, 178

Unamuno, M., 26

Virgil, 49
Vives, Juan Luis, 20
Voltaire, 56

Wallerstein, R., 76, 78, 84
What Is Philosophy? (Ortega y Gassett), 49
Whitaker, C., 179, 180
Wiegert, E., 27
Wittgenstein, Ludwig, 57
Wolberg, L., 45
Wood, H., 81

Zilboorg, Gregory, 20, 73